Wales
Grand Slam
2005

WALES GRAND SLAM 2005

Welsh Rugby Union 2004/05 Patron
Her Majesty The Queen

Undeb Rygbi Cymru 2004/05 Y Noddwraig
Ei Mawrhydi Y Frenhines

Honorary Life Vice-Patron Is-noddwr Mygedol Am Oes
The Rt. Hon. Sir Tasker Watkins V.C., G.B.E., D.L.

President Llywydd
Keith Rowlands

Chairman Cadeirydd
David Pickering

Vice Chairman Is-Gadeirydd
Ken Hewitt

Group Chief Executive Prif – Weithredwr Y Grwp
David Moffett

National Representatives Cynrychiolwyr Cenedlaethol
David Pickering, Howard Watkins, Martin Davies

District Representatives Cynrychiolwyr Dosbarth
Mal Beynon, Geraint Edwards, Humphrey Evans, Brian Fowler, Roy Giddings, Ken Hewitt, Russell Howell, Peredur Jenkins, Alan Jones, John Jones, Anthony John, David Rees, Ray Wilton

Premier Division Representative
Cynrychiolwr Prif Cynghrair
Andy Marinos

Chief Executive, WRU Prif Weithredwr, URC
Steven Lewis

Chief Executive, Millennium Stadium
Prif Weithredwr, Stadiwm Y Mileniwm
Paul Sergeant

Group General Manager, Finance and Administration
Rheolwr Cyffredinol Grwp, Cyllid a Gweinyddiad
Alan Hamer

Millennium Stadium Board of Directors
Bwrdd Cyfarwyddwyr Stadiwm Y Mileniwm
David Pickering (Chairman), David Moffett, Lord Faulkner of Worcester, Byron Davies, Cardiff Council, Ken Hewitt, Martin Davies, Cllr Nigel Howells, Stella Mair Thomas, Helen Conway, Mal Beynon, Geraint Edwards

Grand Slams (9)
1908, 1909, 1911, 1950, 1952, 1971, 1976, 1978, 2005

Triple Crown Winners (18)
1893, 1900, 1902, 1905, 1908, 1909, 1911, 1950, 1952, 1965, 1969, 1971, 1976, 1977, 1978, 1979, 1988, 2005

Five/Six Nations Championship Winners (2)
1994, 2005

Published by:
Profile Sports Media,
5th Floor, Mermaid House,
2 Puddle Dock, London,
EC4V 3DS.

Tel: (+44) 020 7332 2000
Fax: (+44) 020 7332 2001

Printed by: Butler and Tanner Ltd, Frome, Somerset

Copyright Profile Sports Media Limited. All rights reserved. No part of this publication may be reproduced by any means without the written permission of the copyright owners. Although every effort has been made to ensure the accuracy of this publication, the publishers cannot accept responsibility for any errors or omissions. In the interest of independence and impartiality, many features in Wales Grand Slam 2005 have been written on behalf of the publishers by third-party experts. It should be noted that any opinions and recommendations expressed therein are the views of the writers themselves and not those of the WRU.

ISBN: 1 903135 51 6

Distributors:
Vine House
Waldenbury, North Common
Chailey, East Sussex
BN8 4DR.

Tel: (+44) 01825 723398
Fax: (+44) 01825 724188

CONTENTS

FOREWORD by WRU Chairman David Pickering	04
FOREWORD by Wales National Coach Mike Ruddock	06
GERALD DAVIES The legend savours a new dawn in Welsh rugby	08
GARETH THOMAS What's it all about, Alfie?	12
MARTYN WILLIAMS The RBS Player of the Championship reflects on his sensational Six Nations	18
BUILDING THE DREAM The road to Grand Slam glory	24
WALES MATCH REPORTS	
Wales v England	34
Italy v Wales	42
France v Wales	50
Scotland v Wales	58
Wales v Ireland	66
FAN REPORTS Dispatches from the frontline faithful	74
GARETH EDWARDS Pre-match insight and post-match elation from Wales' greatest	82
FINAL TABLE AND STATS	86
WELSH SQUAD PROFILES	88
MIKE RUDDOCK PROFILE	96
RBS 6 NATIONS – OTHER FIXTURES	
France v Scotland	100
Italy v Ireland	102
Scotland v Ireland	104
England v France	106
Scotland v Italy	108
Ireland v England	110
Ireland v France	112
England v Italy	114
Italy v France	116
England v Scotland	118
WELSH GRAND SLAM HISTORY A look back at Wales' illustrious rugby heritage	120

Acknowledgements
The Publishers of Wales Grand Slam 2005 wish to thank Rob Cole from Westgate, Liz Jones from the WRU, Alun Guile and Computacenter for all their assistance.

Photography
The photographs published in Wales Grand Slam 2005 have been contributed by Huw Evans and Getty Images.

Publisher
Eddie Taylor

Managing editor
Owain Jones

Chief sub editor
Stephen Mitchell

Design
Chris Gerrard

Picture editor
Osha Mason

Production manager
Laura Fell

Foreword

David Pickering
WRU Chairman

There is no doubt that the 124th season of the Welsh Rugby Union will go down in history as one of the most successful and crucial in our history. Not only did we win our first Grand Slam in 27 years and bring the RBS 6 Nations title to Wales for the first time, but our game also witnessed seismic changes off the field of play.

It was a season when the rugby world sat up and marvelled at what was happening in Wales, as Mike Ruddock's team helped to restore pride, credibility and respect to our national sport.

As the WRU enters its 125th season we are determined that the successes of the 2004/05 season – which included a third Grand Slam in five years for our Under 21 team – are the beginning, rather than the end, of our renaissance.

In a season of so many highlights, one thing that stood out for me was the style with which the team played. The critics heralded the return of the "Welsh way" during the drive for the Grand Slam. I saw it as the players doing what came naturally to them.

They scored more tries than any other side in the Championship, had one of the best defensive records and, best of all, they played with a constant smile on their faces. That, in turn, ensured the fans, who were equally magnificent throughout the season, had plenty to cheer.

No one who was present at the Millennium Stadium for the wins over England and Ireland at the start and close of the Championship will ever forget the scenes. The whole country was buzzing as Welsh rugby once again gave our proud nation good reason to stand tall.

But we can't rest on our laurels. We have New Zealand, South Africa and Australia coming to challenge us in Cardiff in November, and kick-off the defence of our Six Nations title against England at Twickenham next February – a venue at which we haven't won since 1988.

We are seeking sustained success and that is why we have worked so hard off the field to ensure our structures support the needs of the national side. As well as winning a Grand Slam in 2005, the Union has also won in the boardroom by re-structuring our debt, gaining a £1.6 million Objective 1 funding package for our academy system, selling £2.5 million worth of new debentures and raising £1 million for a new acoustic curtain for the Millennium Stadium.

Welsh rugby has once again proved itself to be a winner – both on and off the field – and this book has been produced to herald our successes. I hope you enjoy it, and I trust we will be able to provide fans of Welsh rugby all over the world with plenty more to shout about in the future.

Foreword
Mike Ruddock

It was an incredible first season to coach Wales. Delivering a first Grand Slam in 27 years was hugely rewarding and satisfying. I guess it has put an enormous amount of pressure on the players and the coaching team for the future – but as a group we welcome it.

When I sat down with the coaching team in June 2004 to plan the way ahead I have to admit I didn't think we would make history in the RBS 6 Nations Championship less than a year on.

I'd admired the style of rugby that Wales had played at the 2003 Rugby World Cup and decided that it would be the foundation of our game. I had also made a conscious decision to promote a style of play that avoided contact as often as possible. Rugby league type defences were dominating and I believed the best way forward was to avoid contact as often as possible, that way the attack could win. That was my message to the players and coaches. I also wanted to promote and encourage our "Welsh Pride" and make the group understand the positive difference that could make. A diary was produced for each player which acted as a protocol or best practice guide. Also included were chapters on Welsh History and the Welsh in Battle. These articles reminded everyone involved about our heritage and culture and the people we represent.

On the technical side we tightened up the pack and the defence, introduced a few new players and right from the outset gave the players a licence to thrill.

And didn't they do just that. The team spirit was fantastic and definitely played a key role in winning the Grand Slam. We were Welsh and we were proud! The Welsh players had been through hard times together and that had made them strong. Now they have an even stronger bond between them, having tasted success.

Everyone keeps asking me about my favourite moment of the Championship, but there were many. Even though I didn't see it, because I'd turned away, that Gavin Henson penalty against England was a crucial moment. Scott Johnson deserved a medal for wearing shorts throughout the game in France when it was absolutely freezing, and the Stephen Jones drop goal in that game was also crucial.

Then there was Gethin Jenkins' charged down try against Ireland and Kevin Morgan's clincher in the same game.

I'll never forget the scenes at the Millennium Stadium after the final whistle had gone against Ireland. It was as though the whole nation was locked inside cheering the team. Nobody wanted to leave and the feeling since then towards the Welsh camp has been sensational and uplifting.

The Welsh fans played a huge role in the winning of the Grand Slam and I hope that this book will give them all something to savour as they reflect on a remarkable few months in the history of Welsh rugby.

It was a pleasure and a privilege to be a part of it, but there is much more to come from this Welsh side and we don't intend to rest on our laurels.

The way of the dragon

Gerald Davies is one of only a handful of Welsh players to have three Grand Slams in his locker. 2005 was the first he can remember as a fan. Here's his view on the new wave of Welsh heroes

The year 2005 was vintage Wales. The year will live long in the memory, the recollections of which will pass colourfully and unforgettably down through the ages. Tall tales will be told when some of us will be nodding quietly by the fire. And, a few years hence, if we come to believe everyone in a white beard who claimed "he was there" then, for sure, we will believe there must have been a million inside the stadium on that sunny spring day back in March 2005. We all want to share in a great Welsh rugby moment.

But the first steps to glory came some time before then.

It was two years earlier under the bright lights of a Sydney night, after 20 years of forgetting and indifference, that Wales first acknowledged its rugby heritage and at last embraced it. Suddenly, without warning, the Welsh team remembered where they came from, felt once more the long-forgotten itch in their soul and discovered the exhilaration of what rugby is meant to define for their country. It had been a long time in coming. But for all of us who were there, we recognised it for what it was: rugby as all of Wales wants the great game to be played.

That mild evening turned what had hitherto been merely ordinary into something quite extraordinary. Inspiration once more coursed in the blood: for those who played and for those, like me, who were privileged to watch. On November 2, 2003 in the World Cup, Australia, Wales and New Zealand were in combat and created such rugby as rightly belonged

09

Previous page: Dwayne Peel evades the French defence. Above: Robert Sidoli gives Reuben Thorne short shrift in the 2003 RWC. Right: Michael Owen breaks into Irish territory

to their long and honourable histories. Welsh pride and respect for tradition had been restored after years of absence and neglect.

Two years later, in 2005, Wales gave even greater cause for celebration. The alchemy of transforming base metal into gold was there for all finally to see. In the Six Nations tournament they won the Championship. And above that they achieved an heroic Grand Slam for the first time in 27 years.

I go back to November 2003, for that's when the first stirrings were witnessed.

For far too long the games between New Zealand and Wales, two great rugby countries, had sadly become one-sided affairs. New Zealand had grown into the habit of treating their close allies in passion for rugby football as someone to dismiss lightly and to be taken not too seriously. New Zealand wanted strong competition. Wales could no longer provide it.

At first it looked like the pattern of recent contests was about to be repeated in the Telstra Stadium match – the final fixture of Pool D. Joe Rokocoko, the marvellous left winger, had scored after two minutes and, we all thought, the sorry tale of Welsh rugby woe was about to revisit us all again. New Zealand were in their stride, the All Black tide unstoppable. We had been here so many times before.

But it was not to be. If, after 36 minutes, New Zealand had scored three tries to Wales' one by Mark Taylor, the worm unexpectedly turned in dramatic fashion. By half time Wales had blazed such a trail of adventure and daring that, with tries

by Sonny Parker and Colin Charvis, they were only four points adrift. Six minutes into the second half, Shane Williams, showing that if Rokocoko could do it then so could he in his different and delightful fashion, had put Wales into the lead.

To achieve this, Wales had played such inspiring rugby that they were given a standing ovation at half-time and, although they were ultimately to lose, the cheers in Sydney went on well into the night. From being the perennial no-hopers, the has-beens of world rugby, Wales were the toast of the town.

I mention this because it's where the Welsh revival began. This was followed a week later by the match against England in Brisbane. Again, Wales were tripping the light fandango and making glorious patterns on Lang Park. The rhythm was quick and clever, ambitious and brave. The ovations went on.

And so it has been ever since.

All this led to the unalloyed joy of the Millennium Stadium on March 19, 2005 when the Six Nations Championship trophy was lifted and the elusive Grand Slam regained.

If November 2003 represented a turning point, it was not until February 2005 that something even more significant began. Wales started winning.

Playing beautiful rugby was fine, but such richness will soon fade if a team is forever losing. Wales' win against England was a major step forward. Not that it was the old enemy, not necessarily because they were the world champions, but rather that Wales had, at last, succeeded in beating one of the strongest rugby teams in the world. They had come so close in the more recent games, but they were never on the right side of the result. This time they were and for the next four matches they never looked back.

To win matches had become essential. Good performances were laudable, but Wales needed to win. No team is credible without success, but Wales' 2005 vintage went further. They not only won matches, they did so in high style.

There is, as I have always maintained, a style of rugby which belongs to Wales. A game of contrasts, of the gelling of hardness with soft touches, of courage with risk, of fleetness of foot with hard shouldered toughness, the poetry of the classroom with the earthly reality of the furnace and the pit. There is passion and instinct, bravery and adventure. This is a great team game of many light and dark shades, but which in Wales insists the single player enjoys his moment of brilliance in the sun. Everywhere there is the dream: the dream of glory.

In 2005 that dream came alive.

"Bliss was it in that dawn to be alive," wrote the Lakeland poet. "But to be young was very heaven."

Let's face it, did not this Welsh team make us all in Wales feel young? After long seasons of failure and despair, the joy returned. Heaven indeed.

The alchemy of transforming base metal into gold was there for all to see

Gareth Thomas

Gareth Thomas has, in less than a year, become one of the nation's most successful skippers. Despite breaking a hand in the game against France, he stayed on with the squad – it's a decision he's glad he made

While it's tempting to say that I always believed Wales could win the Grand Slam in the 2005 season, that wasn't the case. I believed in the players and the coaching and management team, but there are so many things that determine the outcome of an international match. Fate can deal you an unlucky card, a referee can make an error or your team might not play to its full potential. That's why I couldn't honestly say at the start of the RBS 6 Nations campaign that we were going to achieve something a Welsh side had not managed for 27 years.

To find out where our success began you have to go back to some of the bad times we experienced together. You have to respect the foundations that were laid under previous coaches and you have to understand the feeling that existed between the players. We worked hard together and we grew together.

Our preparation for the Championship was meticulous and we examined the strengths and weaknesses of all our opponents. As players, we realised what we needed to work on and everyone did what they had to do. Some Welsh teams in the past had been criticised for not

Mae Gareth Thomas wedi ymddangos fel un o arweinwyr rygbi mwyaf llwyddiannus y genedl o fewn llai na blwyddyn. Er gwaetha torri ei law yn erbyn Ffrainc, fe arhosodd gyda'r garfan. Mae'n falch o'i benderfyniad

Er ei fod yn demtiad i ddweud fy mod wastad wedi credu y bydd Cymru yn ennill y Gamp Lawn yn 2005, nid oedd hwnnw yn hollol gywir. Fe gredais yn y chwaraewyr a'r tîm hyfforddi a rheoli, ond mae 'na gymaint o bethau sy'n effeithio ar ganlyniad gêm ryngwladol. Gall ffawd ddod âg anlwc, gall dyfarnwr wneud camsyniad neu efallai ni all eich tîm chwarae i'w llawn allu. Dyna pam nad oeddwn yn gallu dweud yn onest ar ddechrau ymgyrch Chwe Gwlad RBS ein bod am gyflawni rhywbeth nad oedd tîm o Gymru wedi ei wneud ers 27 mlynedd.

I ddarganfod o ble ddaeth ein llwyddiant, rhaid mynd yn ôl at rai o'r cyfnodau gwael a brofwyd y tymor cynt. Rhaid i chi barchu'r sylfeini a osodwyd gan hyfforddwyr blaenorol a deall y teimladau a fodolodd ymŵsg y chwaraewyr. Fe weithion yn galed gyda'n gilydd ac fe dyfon gyda'n gilydd. Roedd ein paratoadau at y bencampwriaeth yn drwyadl ac fe ddadansoddon gryfderau a gwendidau ein gwrthwynebwyr. Fel chwaraewyr, fe sylweddolon ar beth oedd angen gweithio ac fe wnaeth pawb yr hyn oedd yn rhaid iddynt wneud. Cafodd rhai tîmau Cymru eu beirniadu yn y gorffennol am beidio a gweithio'n ddigon caled, ond fe brofodd aelodau'r garfan hon eu bod yn gewri.

> *I learned a lot about myself while I was injured. Those experiences have made me a better person and captain*

working hard enough, but this squad proved themselves to be Trojans.

Right from the start we knew it was going to be a tough campaign. No team playing three games away from home had won the Grand Slam before. We had to kick-off against the World Cup holders, a team we hadn't beaten in Cardiff for 12 years, and we had to end against a side who had won nine and drawn one of their last 10 games in Wales. And all of these games came in the shortest time frame the Championship had ever been played in – a mere seven weeks. We quickly realised that if we were going to win something, we were going to have to do it the hard way.

That's why we focused on one game at a time, never running ahead of ourselves. That remained the same even as we began to put a run of wins together.

We knew we had a chance of beating England, especially in Cardiff, and I think the whole nation half-expected us to do so. Nevertheless, it still took an incredible kick near the end to win the game. That made all the difference to us. We were quietly confident going to Italy, even though we had lost there two years before, and then there was the game in France. There are few more intimidating places to play than Stade de France and I knew the French players were seething after they had been so heavily criticised for not showing enough adventure in their play – criticism that came after they had beaten Scotland at home and England at Twickenham!

It was a strange afternoon for me, a mixture of highs and lows. We started badly, hung on till half-time and then, in the second period, mounted one of the greatest comebacks in the history of Welsh rugby. It was an awesome performance, yet one to which I wasn't able to contribute fully. When the doctor told me I had broken my thumb just before half-time I was absolutely shell-shocked. I sat in the showers with my head in my hands for the whole of half-time. I simply didn't know what to do with myself.

I felt totally helpless as I watched the second half. It's at times like that you see the

O'r dechrau un fe wyddon roedd am fod yn ymgyrch caled. Nid oedd yr un tîm, wedi ennill y Gamp Lawn o'r blaen wrth chwarae tair gêm oddi cartref. Roedd yn rhaid i ni ddechrau yn erbyn deiliaid Cwpan y Byd, tîm nad oedden wedi curo yng Nghaerdydd ers 12 mlynedd, ac roedd rhaid gorffen yn erbyn tîm a enillodd naw gydag un cyfartal o'i 10 gêm ddiwethaf yng Nghymru. Daeth y gêmau hyn o fewn y cyfnod byrraf y chwaraewyd y bencampwriaeth ynddo erioed, dim ond saith wythnos. Fe sylweddolon yn fuan iawn, os oedden ni am ennill unrhywbeth, roedd rhaid ei wneud y ffordd galed. Dyna pam oedd rhaid ffocysu ar un gêm ar y tro, heb adael i'n hunain ruthro ymlaen. Fe barhaodd hynny hyd yn oed wrth i ni ddechrau ar rediad o fuddugoliaethau.

Fe wyddon ein bod â siawns o guro Lloegr, yn enwedig yng Nghaerdydd, ac rwy'n meddwl roedd y genedl gyfan yn hanner disgwyl i ni. Er hynny, fe gymerodd anferth o gic tua'r diwedd i ennill y gêm. Gwnaeth hwnnw wahaniaeth mawr i ni. Roedden ni'n eithaf hyderus wrth fynd i'r Eidal, er i ni golli yno ddwy flynedd ynghynt, ac yna daeth y gêm yn Ffrainc. Nid oes llawer o loeodd mwy bygythiol i chwarae ynddynt na'r Stade de France ac fe wyddais bod chwaraewyr Ffrainc yn gandryll ar ôl cael eu beirniadu mor hallt am beidio bod mor fentrus yn eu chwarae. Daeth y feirniadeth honno ar ôl iddynt guro'r Alban gartref a Lloegr yn Nhwicenham!

Roedd yn brynhawn rhyfedd i mi, dipyn bach o'r lan a lawr. Fe ddechreuon yn wael, gan ddal ati tan yr egwyl, ac yna dechrau ar un o'r gwrthdrawiadau gorau yn hanes rygbi Cymru yn yr ail hanner. Roedd yn berfformiad anhygoel, ond un nad oeddwn yn gallu cyfrannu iddo'n llawn. Sioc anferth oedd pan ddwedodd y meddyg fy mod i wedi torri fy mawd ar fin yr egwyl. 'Steddais yn y cawod â'm mhen yn fy mhlu trwy gydol yr egwyl. Doedd gen i ddim syniad beth i'w wneud. Teimlais yn gwbwl ddiymadferth wrth wylio'r ail hanner. Ar adegau fel hyn daw gwir gymeriad unigolion a thimoedd i'r

> **Nobody will ever forget the scenes after we had beaten Ireland. It was a fantastic day for the team and the nation**

true character of players and teams shine through, and what happened in that second half in Paris was the start of an incredible few weeks. Martyn Williams grabbed his two tries, Stephen Jones dropped a goal and the whole team tackled like demons. We got ahead, held on and won an incredible victory. From that moment on I think we all knew that this Welsh team was capable of delivering something special.

I had a big decision to make after that game. I had been so proud to captain my country, but now I was unable to play my part. Should I step back and leave the team to get on with things on their own, or stay close and try to help? In the end, it wasn't a difficult decision because I felt so close to the players. We were all accountable

amlwg, a'r hyn a ddigwyddodd yn yr ail hanner ym Mharis oedd yn ddechreuad i wythnosau anhygoel. Cipiodd Matryn Williams ei ddau gais, ciciodd Stephen Jones gôl adlam a thaclodd y tîm cyfan fel diawlied. Aethom ar y blaen, cadw'r blaenoriaeth gan ennill buddugoliaeth anghredadwy. O'r foment honno dwi'n credu y gwyddom i gyd bod y tîm Cymreig hwn â'r gallu i gyflawni rhywbeth sbesial.

Roedd gen i benderfyniad mawr i'w wneud ar ôl y gêm honno. Rown i mor falch o fod yn gapten dros fy ngwlad, ond nawr nid oeddwn yn gallu chwarae fy rhan. A ddyla' i gamu'n ôl a gadael i'r tîm barhau ar ei ben ei hun, neu a ddyla' i aros a cheisio cynorthwyo? Yn y pen draw, nid oedd yn benderfyniad anodd i'w wneud, gan fy mod yn teimlo mor agos at y chwaraewyr. Roedden ni i gyd yn atebol i'n gilydd a doeddwn i ddim am eu gadael i lawr mewn unrhyw ffordd. Felly dyma fi'n teithio gyda nhw i'r Alban ac yn aros gyda'r hyfforddiant cyn y gêm dyngedfennol yn erbyn Iwerddon.

Rhaid i mi ddweud mai dyna'r wythnosau mwyaf caled i mi ddioddef fel campwr, ond rwy' mor falch fy mod i wedi cefnogi'r bois. Dysgais lawer am fy hun a'm tîm yn ystod fy anaf ac rwy'n teimlo bod y profiadau hynny, pa bynnag mor galed yr oeddent ar lefel personol, wedi fy ngwneud yn well berson a chapten. Nawr gallaf uniaethu gyda'r sawl sydd ar y fainc ac ar yrion y tîm ac wnai ddim anghofio hynny.

Wn i ddim os oedd fy mhresenoldeb yn gymorth neu'n rwystr, ond rwy'n cofio sgwrsio'n dawel gyda Kevin Morgan cyn gêm Yr Alban. A beth wnaeth e ar ôl hynny? Chwarae allan o'i groen ym Murrayfield, gan sgorio dau gais, ac yn a un arall yn erbyn Iwerddon.

Ar ôl y fuddugoliaeth yn yr Alban, rown i'n tybio nad oedd unrhywbeth yn gallu ein rhwystro yn erbyn Iwerddon yng Nghaerdydd. Ymddangosowyd bod y sgript wedi cael ei sgrifennu i ni ac roedd yna awyrgylch o hyder tawel yn y garfan. Wrth ddeffro ar fore'r gêm gyda'r haul yn tywynnu, teilais yn fwy hyderus fyth.

Bydd neb yn anghofio'r golygfeydd ar ôl curo Iwerddon. Diwrnod rhyfeddol oedd

to each other and I didn't want to let them down in any way. So, I travelled with them to Scotland and stayed around the training camp in the build-up to the Grand Slam decider against Ireland.

I have to say they were among the toughest few weeks I've ever encountered as a sportsman, but I'm so glad I backed the boys. I learned a lot about myself and my team while I was injured and I feel those experiences, however difficult they might have been on a personal level, have made me a better person and captain. Now I know exactly how the people on the replacements bench and the fringes of the team feel and I won't forget that.

I'm not sure if my presence was a help or a hindrance, but I can remember going up to Kevin Morgan before the game in Scotland and having a few quiet words in his ear. And what did he do after that? He played a blinder at Murrayfield, scoring two tries, and then running in another against Ireland.

After the win in Scotland I didn't think anything could stop us against Ireland in Cardiff. It seemed the script had been written for us and there was a quiet air of confidence in the camp. When I woke up on the day of the game and saw the sun shining, I felt even more confident.

Nobody will ever forget the scenes after we had beaten Ireland. It was a fantastic day not just for the team, but for the whole nation. This team did it for their families, friends and their country, and to see so many people smiling after our victory was fantastic.

I'm sure the feeling of winning the Grand Slam in 2005 will simply get better and better as we get older. It's an achievement that can never be taken away from the players involved. But, as professional sportsmen, we now have to face fresh challenges – like the All Blacks, Springboks and Wallabies in the autumn, and opening our defence of the RBS 6 Nations title against England at Twickenham.

There is much more to come from this Welsh team, and those are the games that are going to bring out the best in us.

e, nid yn unig i'r tîm ond i'r genedl gyfan. Gwnaeth y tîm y gamp er mwyn eu teuluoedd, ffrindiau a'u gwlad, ac roedd yn wefreiddiol gweld cymaint o bobl yn gwenu.

Rwy'n siwr bydd y teimlad o ennill y Gamp Lawn yn 2005 yn gwella wrth fynd yn hŷn. Ni all unrhyw un gymryd y gamp oddi ar y chwaraewyr oedd yn rhan ohoni. ond fel campwyr proffesiynol, rhaid i ni wynebu herion newydd – fel y Crysau Duon, y Springboks a'r Walabîs yn yr Hydref ac agor amddiffyniad ein pencampwriaeth RBS o'r Chwe Gwlad yn erbyn Lloegr yn Nhwicenham. Mae yna gymaint yn fwy i ddod o'r tîm hwn o Gymru a rheiny yw'r gêmau a fydd yn tynnu'r gorau ohonom fel grŵp.

Martyn Williams

The RBS 6 Nations Player of the Championship discusses the emotions experienced within the Welsh camp and explains his remarkable form in this year's momentous Grand Slam campaign

For me, the Grand Slam season just got better and better. At the start of the year I was merely hoping to make the 22 for the Championship, dreading that my 50th cap would come with a final flourish of a few minutes in one of the games. Then disaster struck and I picked up a neck injury that was supposed to rule me out of at least the first two matches. All of a sudden it seemed as though everything was in the balance.

That's when the unseen teamwork in the Welsh camp came shining through for me. The doctors and physios worked tirelessly on my injury, the coaches constantly encouraged me and the rest of the players supported me through the tough times. That's how it was for everyone in the squad – we trained hard together, we sweated together, we had fun together and we helped each other through the good and bad times.

It meant the good times were great and the bad times were easier than they might have been. In the end, I was able to get fit enough to play against England. I led the team out at the Millennium Stadium to mark my 50th cap and we won the game. Talk about a perfect start to the Championship!

France was fantastic, with those two tries at the start of the second half,

Mae Chwaraewr Gorau Pencampwriaeth RBS y Chwe Gwlad yn trafod yr emosiynau a brofwyd o fewn carfan Cymru ac yn egluro ei berfformiadau arbennig yn ystod ymgyrch y Gamp Lawn eleni

I mi, daeth tymor y Gamp Lawn yn well bob munud. Ar ddechrau'r flwyddyn 'rown i ddim ond yn gobeithio cyrraedd y garfan o 22 ar gyfer y bencampwriaeth, gan ofni mai dim ond ar ddiwedd un o'r gêmau y byddwn yn ennill fy 50fed cap. Yna daeth trychineb; anafais fy ngwddf a oedd i fod fy atal rhag chwarae yn o leiaf y ddwy gêm cyntaf. Yn sydyn roedd popeth yn y fantol.

Dyna'r adeg pan ddaeth cydweithrediad anweledig carfan Cymru yn amlwg i mi. Gweithiodd y meddygon a'r ffysios yn ddyfal ar yr anaf, annogodd yr hyfforddwyr arnaf a chefais gefnogaeth y chwaraewr trwy'r cyfnod caled. Dyna sut oedd i bawb yn y garfan – hyfforddi'n galed, chwysu, cael hwyl a helpu gyda'n gilydd trwy'r cyfnodau da a gwael.

Golygodd hyn bod y cyfnodau da yn grêt a'r cyfnodau gwael yn haws i'w trin. Yn y diwedd, rown i'n ddigon iach i chwarae yn erbyn Lloegr. Arweiniais y tîm allan ar Faes y Milflwydd i ddathlu fy 50fed cap ac enillon ni'r gêm. Sôn am ddechreuad perffaith i'r bencampwriaeth!

Roedd gêm Ffrainc yn ffantastig, gyda'r ddau gais ar ddechrau'r ail hanner, ac yna daeth tlws Seren y Gêm yn annisgwyladwy yn erbyn Yr Eidal ar ôl cais cyfrwys arall.

Roedd gêm Yr Alban yn llafurus – sut arall fyddech chi'n teimlo ar ôl chwarae

MARTYN WILLIAMS

> *The achievement will stay with us for the rest of our lives, but we don't see it as career defining. This has to be just the start*

and then came a thoroughly unexpected Man-of-the-Match trophy in Italy after another sneaky try. Scotland was exhausting – how else would you feel after playing in a game in which the ball stayed in play for 43.5 minutes – and Ireland was exhilarating.

The margin between winning and losing at international level is so small that you have to ride your luck when you can and hang tough when you feel things slipping away. They say, "cometh the hour, cometh the man", and in every game throughout the Championship we had someone in the team who was prepared to step forward and make an impact.

For Gavin Henson in the closing moments against England, read Stephen Jones in Paris. For Shane Williams in Italy, think Ryan Jones in Scotland. And as for Ireland, who will ever forget that charge down by Gethin Jenkins that brought us the first-half try that settled our nerves.

In many ways it still hasn't sunk in that we have finally won the Six Nations title and taken the Grand Slam for the first time in 27 years. I was only just walking and talking when the "Gods of 1978" made it three Grand Slams in eight years. Now I have not only seen Wales scale the same heights, but I've also been a part of it. The achievement will stay with us for the rest of our lives, but we don't see it as career defining. This has to be just the start.

Much of the season remains a blur, but there are a few things that have stuck in the mind and continue to raise a smile. Like the motivational tapes produced by our analyst Alun Carter. They are a blend of hype, hope and fun and they always play a part in getting us ready over the closing 24 hours. We had the Amarillo music playing over some of our training routines, Gareth Thomas being compared to Sharp Teeth from Wallace and Gromit and some snatch footage of Mike Ruddock sidestepping his way to his car after training when he thought nobody could see him. As if a back-row man could sidestep properly! There were a few mewn gêm lle'r oedd y bêl yn fyw am 43.5 munud – ac roedd Iwerddon yn llawn cynnwrf.

Mae'r ffin rhwng ennill a cholli ar lefel rhyngwladol mor denau, mae angen defnyddio'ch lwc pryd y gallech a dal ati'n ddygn pan fydd pethau o chwith. Yn ôl y dywediad, daw'r awr ac fe ddaw'r dyn ac ym mhob gêm trwy gydol y bencampwriaeth roedd gennym rywun yn y tîm oedd yn barod i ddangos y ffordd.

Am Gavin Henson yn y munudau olaf yn erbyn Lloegr darllener Stephen Jones ym Mharis. Am Shane Williams yn Yr Eidal, meddylier am Ryan Jones yn Yr Alban. Ac am Iwerddon, pwy all beidio anghofio'r ymyrraeth ar y gic gan Gethin Jenkins a ddaeth â'r cais yn yr hanner cyntaf i setlo'n nerfau.

Mewn sawl ffordd nid ydyw wedi suddo i mewn ein bod ni wedi ennill pencampwriaeth y Chwe Gwlad o'r diwedd ac wedi cipio'r Gamp Lawn am y tro cyntaf mewn 27 mlynedd. Doeddwn ddim ond yn dechrau cerdded a siarad pan gafodd Duwiau 1978 y Gamp Lawn deirgwaith mewn wyth mlynedd. Nawr dwi ddim yn unig wedi gweld Cymru'n cyrraedd yr un nod, ond dwi wedi bod yn rhan ohono hefyd. Bydd y gamp yn aros gyda ni trwy'n hoes, ond nid y diwedd yw hyn. Hwn yw'r man cychwyn.

Mae llawer o'r tymor braidd yn anghof, ond mae ambell beth gwirion wedi aros ar gof. Fel y tapiau i'n cymell gan ein dadansoddwr Alun Carter. Cymysgedd o heip, gobaith a hwyl ydynt ac maen nhw'n wastad yn ein helpu i baratoi dros y 24 awr olaf. Cawsom fiwsig Amarillo yn chwarae yn ystod ambell sesiwn hyfforddiant, Gareth Thomas yn cael ei gymharu â Sharp Teeth o Wallace a Gromit a lluniau dirgel o Mike Ruddock yn ochrgamu i'w gar gan feddwl byddai neb yn ei weld. Rhengôlwr yn ochrgamu! Roedd yna enghreifftiau o beth i'w beidio a gwneud, fel Adam Jones yn ceisio trosi o'r ystlys ac ambell eiliad difrifol hefyd. Roedd hyn oll yn gymorth wrth baratoi.

Ers curo Iwerddon ac ennill y Gamp Lawn mae sawl un wedi gofyn beth oedd

sequences of what not to do, as demonstrated by Adam Jones trying to kick a conversion off the touchline, and some serious moments as well. It all hit the spot and it all made a tiny difference.

Since we beat Ireland and won the Grand Slam every other person has asked me what made the difference from previous seasons. After all, we are more or less the same group of players who over the previous two seasons conceded a Six Nations whitewash, got beaten in Italy and quite often failed to raise a smile for our fans. Well, the success of 2005 was a long time in the making and has to be put down to hard work, more hard work and even more hard work. As a group of players we never gave

yn wahanol o gymharu eleni â thymhorau blaenorol. Wedi'r cwbwl rydym yr un grwp o chwaraewyr, fwy neu lai, a ddioddefodd wyngalchiad yn y Chwe Gwlad, a gollodd yn Yr Eidal ac yn eithaf aml wedi methu rhoi gwên ar wynebau'n cefnogwyr dros y ddwy flynedd ddiwethaf. Wel, roedd llwyddiant 2005 yn ganlyniad o waith caled a chaletach dros dymor hir. Fel grwp o chwaraewyr nid oeddem am roi'r gorau iddi ac roeddem wastad yn credu bod gennym y talent i gystadlu â'r gwledydd eraill. Roedd llawer o'r newid yn ganlyniad o symudiad yn ein agwedd seicolegol a'r ffaith ein bod ni'n ennill. Pwy a ŵyr beth fyddai wedi digwydd i'n tymor petai cic Gavin Henson wedi methu yn erbyn Lloegr.

up on ourselves or each other and we always believed we had the talent to compete with the other nations. A lot of the change was due to a shift in our psychological approach and even more has to be put down to winning. Who knows what might have happened to our season if Gavin's kick had gone wide against England.

But it went the right side of the post, the nation got behind us like never before and we gathered more and more momentum. It got to the stage in the Grand Slam game against Ireland where we almost felt we couldn't be beaten. There is a corridor in the WRU training headquarters that is about 60 metres long and in the week of the Irish match it was full from floor to ceiling with good luck messages from Welsh fans. There were flags sent to us from some Welsh soldiers in Iraq, a message from the Prince of Wales and heartfelt good wishes from proud Welsh men and women all over the world. It was fantastic and a huge motivational tool for everyone in the camp.

In most international games you get a big five minutes of noise at the start and then everything calms down, but the mood in the Millennium Stadium for the game against Ireland was quite different. It was as though there was a party atmosphere right from the kick-off. The weather was great, the fans were awesome and we certainly fed off their energy. And if the support at the start was incredible, then the noise and scenes at the end were unforgettable. It is moments like that that make the Millennium Stadium the greatest theatre for sport in the world.

The Saturday night after winning the Grand Slam was pretty special, but the day after, when we all went out and let our hair down, was even better. Having been through so many hard times together, I think we appreciated even more the success that we had previously only dreamed of achieving. It all became a wonderful reality as we sat down and relaxed together as a squad, finally able to enjoy a beer or two after seven weeks of intense concentration and physical commitment.

What we achieved in the first quarter of 2005 will forever live in our minds, although as professional sportsmen we know we have to shift our focus forward pretty quickly to the challenges that lie ahead. We may have proved we can once again compete with the best teams in the world, but we know that the legendary status that some might seek to put on us is still a long way off. Our aim is to use the 2005 Grand Slam as the stepping stone for sustained success – four or five years of things to shout about for the greatest fans in world.

Ond fe aeth i ochr gywir y postyn, daeth y genedl i'n cefnogi a chawsom fwy a mwy o fomentwm. Daeth i'r pwynt yng ngêm y Gamp Lawn yn erbyn Iwerddon lle roeddem yn credu bod neb yn gallu ein curo. Mae yna gyntedd ym mhencadlys hyfforddi URC sydd yn 60 metr o hyd ac yn yr wythnos cyn gêm Iwerddon roedd y waliau'n llawn o negeseuon lwc dda gan gefnogwyr Cymru. Danfonodd milwyr o Gymry yn Irac faneri atom, neges oddi wrth Tywysog Cymru a dymuniadau gorau o waelod calonnau Cymry dros y byd. Roedd e'n ffantastig ac yn hwb mawr i bawb yn y garfan.

Yn y rhan fwyaf o gêmau rhyngwladol cewch bum munud swnllyd dros ben ar y dechrau ac yna bydd pethau yn tewi, ond roedd yr hwyl ar Faes y Milflwydd yng ngêm Iwerddon yn gwbl gwahanol. Roedd yn debyg i barti o'r dechrau. Roedd y tywydd yn braf, a'r cefnogwyr yn ei morio hi a ninnau yn bwydo ar eu hegni. Os oedd y gefnogaeth yn anghredadwy ar y dechrau, roedd y sŵn a'r olygfa ar y diwedd yn ddiangof tu hwnt. Adegau fel hyn sydd yn gwneud Maes y Milflwydd y theatr gampau gorau yn y byd.

Roedd y nos Sadwrn ar ôl ennill y Gamp Lawn yn eitha' sbesial, ond drannoeth, pan aethom i gyd allan i wledda, roedd e'n well byth. Wedi mynd trwy cyfnodau caled gyda'n gilydd, dwi'n meddwl i ni werthfawrogi'n llwyddiant fwyfwy. Daeth yn wireddiad rhyfeddol wrth i ni eistedd ac ymlacio o'r diwedd fel carfan, gan fwynhau ambell i gwrw ar ôl saith wythnos o ganolbwyntio dwys ac ymroddiad ffisegol.

Bydd yr hyn a gyflawnwyd yn ystod chwarter cyntaf 2005 yn aros am byth yn ein cof, er fel campwyr proffesiynol, fe wyddom y bydd rhaid i ni ganolbwyntio yn eithaf cyflym ar herion y dyfodol. Efallai rydym wedi dangos ein bod yn gallu cystadlu gyda'r gorau yn y byd, ond fe wyddom bod y statws chwedlonol bydd ambell un am roi i ni yn bell i ffwrdd. Ein nod yw i ddefnyddio Camp Lawn 2005 fel cam at lwyddiant mwy cyson – pedair neu bum mlynedd i gefnogwyr gorau'r byd rygbi i frolio amdanynt.

Building the dream

Chris Deary charts how, in just two seasons, Wales have gone from a Six Nations wooden spoon to a glorious Grand Slam

BUILDING THE DREAM

The 2003 Six Nations Championship was one to forget for Wales: five defeats, no wins and 144 points scored against, all adding up to Wales relieving Italy of the wooden spoon for the first time since the competition was expanded in 2000.

Who would have thought then that, within the space of only two years, Wales would have recaptured the halcyon days of the 1970s by winning their first Grand Slam in 27 years?

The transformation did not happen overnight, nor was it without its false dawns. The appointment of New Zealander Graham Henry as coach in 1998 brought renewed optimism after a decade of disappointment interrupted only by a Five Nations triumph in 1994. Test victories over England, France and South Africa in Henry's first few months in the job were followed by a creditable showing at the 1999 World Cup – where they were eliminated in the quarter-finals by the eventual tournament champions Australia – and in the inaugural Six Nations the following year.

But in the 2001/02 season, cracks began to appear. Defeats to Argentina and Ireland (a record 51-10 loss) represented a major step backwards, and by February a dejected Henry had resigned.

His successor, fellow Kiwi Steve Hansen – who had originally been brought in under Henry to coach the forwards – vowed to continue the necessary restructuring, and many credit him with instilling the side with some southern hemisphere fitness and professionalism.

"Rugby is a basic game where you have to learn to crawl before you walk, and to walk before you can run," he once said. "We have got to learn to crawl first. We need some inner belief."

Yet results showed little sign of improvement. An 11-game losing streak, which incorporated that disastrous Six Nations campaign of 2003, was ended only by victories over Romania and Scotland, and there were heavy suggestions that Hansen approached the World Cup from a prominent seat in the last chance saloon.

The turning point, in terms of performances at least, was that 2003 World Cup in Australia.

After uninspired, if satisfactory, victories against Canada, Tonga and Italy, Wales took on New Zealand in the final pool game having already progressed to the quarter-finals. They had nothing to lose and Hansen fielded a "weakened side" in readiness for England. It was the incisive running of then third-choice scrum-half Shane Williams that lit up the group game against New

Previous page: Charvis raises the troops at the RWC 2003. Left: Shanklin helps stop the Kiwi machine in its tracks

Above: "Alfie" evades the English defence in the World Cup quarter-final. Following page: Henson begins to show his class in the Autumn Series

Zealand, from which Wales emerged with their heads held high, despite a 53-37 defeat. And Wales took that confidence into their quarter-final against England, with three glorious first-half tries giving them the lead, before England's forward pressure and the metronomic boot of Johnny Wilkinson kicked the eventual winners into the semis.

The man brought in to tighten up the forward play was actually having more success in getting Wales to run the ball, but the transformation back to the "Welsh way" of playing would only be completed with a Welshman at the helm.

After the 2004 Six Nations – in which Wales registered entertaining wins over Italy and Scotland but struggled to find any consistency – the Kiwi reign came to an end, with Steve Hansen being given a warm farewell at the Millennium Stadium. Llanelli Scarlets director of rugby Gareth Jenkins and Harlequins boss Mark Evans were both shortlisted for the job of national coach, but the Welsh Rugby Union instead surprised many by appointing Mike Ruddock, former coach of the Wales A side and assistant coach to Alec Evans in the 1995 World Cup.

WRU chairman David Pickering said at the time: "We explored every avenue to get the best possible man for the job. We put him through the same selection

> I was really impressed by their ambition, their style and the tempo at which they delivered it

BUILDING THE DREAM

process as the others and he presented the best case. We had an absolute duty to seek out the best potential candidates and we had to leave no stone unturned."

Ruddock signalled his intentions when he announced that Wales had a "licence to thrill", and a 42-0 win over the Barbarians in his first game in charge suggested the WRU had made the right decision. But defeats against Argentina and South Africa last summer meant the jury was still out by the time of the Autumn Series at the back end of 2004.

The series began with a narrow 36-38 defeat to South Africa. But like the game against New Zealand in the World Cup, the performance offered more than the result, especially considering the heavy defeat meted out by the same opposition earlier in the year – and the fact that the Springboks had established themselves as the southern hemisphere's top side by winning the Tri-Nations Championship.

Most encouraging of all was the way Wales finished the game on the front foot. As Eddie Butler wrote in *The Guardian*: "Deep into stoppage time, Wales unleashed a scrummage that shot the South Africans skyward and backwards. Dwayne Peel, one of the stars of the afternoon, nipped in behind the retreating legs, picked the ball up and scored Wales' third try. It was a perfect end to an encouraging performance on home soil."

At one stage in the first half, Wales had been 23-6 down, but they demonstrated the never-say-die attitude that would come to the fore against both the English and French in the forthcoming Six Nations by battling back to within two points of the South Africans at the final whistle.

Ruddock said after the game: "I was really impressed with the players; by how they approached the game after falling behind – their ambition, their style of play and the tempo at which they delivered it."

Next up were Romania, who were swept aside with ten tries, four of them from Tom Shanklin. The biggest plus from Ruddock's point of view, though, was the performance of the defence.

Against South Africa, Wales had demonstrated their willingness to play expansive, entertaining rugby, but questions remained about the durability of the pack.

"It was a good defensive workout," said Ruddock after watching the comfortable 66-7 win. "We only had to complete 74 tackles against South Africa and surprisingly against Romania we made 144 tackles. We showed we can attack with our ten tries, but also that we can defend and absorb pressure for a sustained period on our own line."

Those defensive qualities would be tested to the max against their next opponents New Zealand.

But if the closeness of the scoreline against South Africa could be put down to the visitors still finding their feet on the tour, the same could not be said against the All Blacks. Wales were 14-13 up at the break and maybe should have gone on to win after Ma'a Nonu was sent to the sin bin in the second-half after flooring Gavin Henson with a late tackle.

In the end, the result was another painful defeat, 25-26, but there was no obvious gulf, with Wales' turning in another impressive performance. Defeat by just a single point against a team they have not beaten since 1953 represented a significant achievement and offered genuine hope for the future.

Ruddock felt his side would have been victorious with a little luck. "It was a game we felt we should have won," he said. "It was different to the South Africa match where we had to chase the game after an indifferent start. We went out there with the attitude that we wanted to boss the game from the off."

The fitness and work ethic instilled by Henry and Hansen was beginning to pay dividends, but against the Kiwis there was another quality on display – a renewed sense of Welsh pride. After the visitors had completed their Haka, tenor Wynne

> **The 80 minutes on the field are a reflection of the hours and hours we put in on the training pitch**

BUILDING THE DREAM

Evans led the home crowd with an incredible, spine-tingling rendition of *Bread of Heaven*.

"The crowd were absolutely awesome," Ruddock said. "I thought it was a terrific response. It drew upon our Welsh culture and heritage and everything we're trying to get across. We produced a booklet for the squad detailing Welsh history and culture and they've responded to that with re-ignited passion."

The visit of Japan, six days later, hardly represented a similar test, but the attacking flair was again on show as Wales set a new record for their highest winning margin with a 98-0 win (beating the record of 102-11 from the win over Portugal ten years earlier).

Four-try hero Colin Charvis said after the game: "There is a great work ethic and there is a lot of competition in the squad to get the jersey on your back. The 80 minutes on the field are a reflection of the hours and hours we put in on the training pitch and in the gym. Everyone is determined to do well and we are all working very hard. It's still a bitter pill to swallow that we lost so narrowly to South Africa and New Zealand, but we are now looking forward to the Six Nations."

Collectively there was much by which to be encouraged, and there were also some good individual performances. Henson cemented his place for the No 12 jersey with two tries against South Africa and 14 conversions from 14 attempts against Japan, while Michael Owen, Gethin Jenkins and Mefin Davies also had impressive campaigns.

At the end of the Autumn Series the IRB World Rankings still had Wales outside a top six that included their Six Nations rivals England, France and Ireland. But there was cautious optimism, as Ruddock reflected in his summing up of the series.

"We delivered on what we wanted – four big performances, and a tempo and excitement that would bring the Welsh public in. We're not world-beaters. There's a long way to go and a lot of hard work ahead, but we've made progress."

That hard work meant finding a way of turning performances into victories. "I believe we are an improved team and, on our day, we can give anyone a game," said Ruddock. "But we have to learn to win tight games now. We are not going to blow our own trumpet."

By the end of the Six Nations, there would be plenty of people willing to do that for them.

RBS 6 NATIONS
Steps to glory

Wales v England	34
Italy v Wales	42
France v Wales	50
Scotland v Wales	58
Wales v Ireland	66

Wales 11 England 9

Millennium Stadium

Saturday, February 5, 2005

Attendance: 74,197

Previous page: Gavin Henson stretches his legs. Left: Shane Williams looks for the gap. Right: Adam Jones and Henson savour victory

WALES v ENGLAND

The Six Nations Championship was turned on its head by Wales with a gripping last-ditch victory against England for the first time in Cardiff since 1993. England had edged to a precarious one-point lead, before Gavin Henson, starting his first Six Nations game, landed a penalty, four minutes from time, to clinch an 11-9 victory.

Wales came into this first game of the Six Nations series quietly optimistic, after much improved performances against South Africa and New Zealand in the autumn. England's team news only added to their hopes. Blighted by a series of retirements, including Martin Johnson and Lawrence Dallaglio, and injuries to Jonny Wilkinson, Mike Tindall and Will Greenwood, the Chariot was limping somewhat. It was commonly consented that this was Wales' best opportunity in a decade to beat England. Mike Ruddock was underplaying his team's chances, stating that England were a fine side and reigning World Champions, but privately he must have sensed a chance. The scene was set and, with Welsh fans in full voice at the Millennium Stadium, the atmosphere reached fever pitch.

The game had several defining moments, none more so than the decision by Andy Robinson to blood Mathew Tait, a promising 18-year-old from Newcastle. This selection seemed to be a chronic mismatch with Gavin Henson – Wales' very own pin-up – who welcomed Tait to Test rugby by stopping him in his tracks early in the game, his good looks belying a steely resolve. Henson, a relative unknown outside the Principality before the game, was about to see his star go into orbit.

The match was a fairly scrappy, close-knit affair – a typical opening Six Nations game. The first half saw Wales make most of the running with their backline asking questions of the English defence. They opened the scoring in the 10th minute with some

WALES v ENGLAND

> **You never need any greater motivation than to see a white shirt in front of you!**
> *Martyn Williams*

> **Wales against England isn't just a game – this is rugby warfare. No prisoners taken, no holds barred. Last men standing get the glory**
> *Robert Jones*

> **I'm just so pleased for all the boys because we battled it out and didn't let our heads drop when they went ahead**
> *Mike Ruddock*

> **I've given myself a bit of a row about being yellow-carded. Having said that I have been sent to my room by my mum for a lot worse**
> *Gareth Thomas*

Left: The 12-year wait for a home win against England is over. Following page: The Millennium Stadium erupts

quickfire handling from Henson and Michael Owen, leaving the English defence stretched and little Shane Williams scampered over for a try in the corner. The rest of the half saw penalty misses from both kickers.

The next key moment came before half-time with the score standing at 8-3. Wales had England under pressure on their own line and at the resulting maul, Danny Grewcock appeared to boot Dwayne Peel on the head, in what most thought was a patently violent manner. Wales would surely have had a penalty, had captain Gareth Thomas not raced over to remonstrate with Grewcock and give him a retaliatory shove. Both were shown the yellow card and trudged off to cool down.

In the second-half, England started to improve, with Kay and pantomime villain Grewcock being increasingly used as battering rams to drive up the middle of the park. Charlie Hodgson kept England in the game by striking a sweet penalty to put his side ahead 9-8 with only seven minutes to go – leaving Wales, who had had the best of the game, staring at another cruel defeat. It was now or never for the home team. A kick and chase by replacement Gareth Cooper swept Wales upfield and forced Jason Robinson into giving away a penalty in the 76th minute. Stephen Jones hadn't been having the best of days in front of the posts, and at 44 metres from a tight angle, he wasn't sure he had the range. Welsh fans, sensing Jones's conundrum, started chanting Henson's name, and he stepped up, hunched over the ball and struck it sweetly through the posts to send the crowd into raptures. The lead seemed to give Wales renewed impetus and they finished off the match much the stronger side, leaving England to slope off the pitch having lost their first game against Wales in six years.

Wales		England
Gareth Thomas(c)	15	Jason Robinson(c)
Hal Luscombe	14	Mark Cueto
Tom Shanklin	13	Mathew Tait
Gavin Henson	12	Jamie Noon
Shane Williams	11	Josh Lewsey
Stephen Jones	10	Charlie Hodgson
Dwayne Peel	9	Matt Dawson
Gethin Jenkins	1	Graham Rowntree
Mefin Davies	2	Steve Thompson
Adam Jones	3	Julian White
Brent Cockbain	4	Danny Grewcock
Rob Sidoli	5	Ben Kay
Dafydd Jones	6	Chris Jones
Martyn Williams	7	Andy Hazell
Michael Owen	8	Joe Worsley

Replacements: Gareth Cooper for Peel (61), Ryan Jones for D Jones (64), Kevin Morgan for Luscombe (65), Jonathan Thomas for Cockbain (73), John Yapp for A Jones (74)
Sin Bin: G Thomas (37)
Try: S Williams
Pens: S Jones, Henson

Replacements: James Forrester for Worsley (41-43), Phil Vickery for Rowntree (57), Olly Barkley for Tait (60), Harry Ellis for Dawson (65), Steve Borthwick for Grewcock (67), Graham Rowntree for White (77)
Sin Bin: Grewcock (37)
Pens: Hodgson 3

Referee: Steve Walsh (New Zealand)

MATCH STATISTICS

Wales		England
7	Scrums Won	8
1	Scrums Lost	0
13	Penalties Conceded	10
66	Tackles Made	55
8	Missed Tackles	4
89	% Tackles Completed	93
19	Errors Made	22
6	Turn Overs Won	3
99	Passes Completed	63
29	Possessions Kicked	26
22	% Possessions Kicked	29
9	Poss. Kicked To Touch	13

RBS Man of the Match: Gavin Henson

The great Welsh hope, Gavin Henson, more than lived up to his pre-match billing, inspiring a famous victory against the old enemy for the boys in red. With boots of silver and nerves of steel he slotted over a crucial late penalty from 44 metres to send a nation into celebration mode. His contribution and commitment throughout the match were colossal, combining clever chips with some incendiary touch-finders that had the opposition reeling. Henson played his part in Wales' try, offloading to Michael Owen, who then fed Shane Williams, and few will forget his imperious dumping of fellow young-gun Mathew Tait in what was a truly majestic performance.

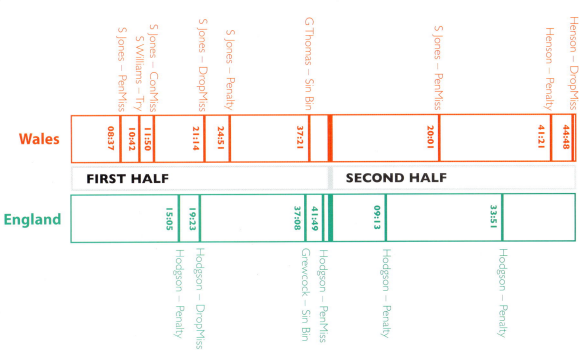

Italy 8 Wales 38

Stadio Flaminio

Saturday, February 12, 2005

Attendance: 25,660

ITALY v WALES

Previous page: Gavin Henson waves goodbye. Left: Brent Cockbain powers on. Right: Gareth Cooper leaps into action

After the stirring victory over England at the Millennium Stadium the previous weekend, the prospect of a trip to Rome and the homely Stadio Flaminio wouldn't have held too many fears for a side with rising confidence and self-belief. That said, Italy had played with surprising steel and enterprise in the opening encounter with Ireland, unsettling the pre-tournament favourites with punishing defence and a highly combative pack. Wales were careful to guard against complacency, with many surviving coaching staff and players still smarting from a painful 30-22 loss at the hands of the Azzurri in 2003.

Thankfully, after just six minutes, some Shane Williams trickery on the 10-metre line set up the attack that culminated with a Michael Owen break and looping pass for Jonathan Thomas to score his debut try. Stephen Jones converted and Wales, seemingly, were on their way. But just when Gavin Henson was set to penetrate deep into the Italian half, having skipped away from Fabio Ongaro and Walter Pozzebon and sprinted up the touchline, his delicate chip behind the defence was retrieved by Luciano Orquera who outstripped the Welsh defence for a full 50 metres to steal a highly opportunistic score. Suddenly, with just 11 minutes on the clock, it was 7-5.

Ten minutes later, though, Henson's boot had a more positive effect. Firstly, his prodigious kick into the Italian 22 forced a five-metre scrum, and when the ball reappeared in the open following a succession of rucks, a Henson chip this time succeeding in finding a leaping Tom Shanklin, who just managed to exert sufficient downward pressure on the ball when he returned to earth. Any lingering doubts about Wales' ability to kill off the game were banished on the stroke of half-time when Martyn Williams collected

> **We decided we were going to be in charge from the first minute**
> *Mike Ruddock*

> **It was great to see that so many Welsh fans had made the trip. They certainly made their presence felt**
> *Rob Sidoli*

> **I don't know if teams will fear us now, but they will certainly respect us**
> *Stephen Jones*

> **We kicked away too much loose ball and Wales have got players who can punish that. They are an excellent team that play spectacular rugby**
> *John Kirwan, Italy coach*

ITALY v WALES

a pass from Hal Luscombe, whose angled run took him clear of the Italian defence, to score at the foot of a post. At 19-5, the game was as good as sealed.

The second half confirmed the gap in the two sides' conditioning and quality. The defensive resolve that was so in evidence against Ireland evaporated at the feet of Shane Williams, and with 15 minutes of the new period gone, he evaded the entire Italian midfield to feed Jonathan Thomas and set up a maiden score for Brent Cockbain. A fifth try soon followed as Shane Williams capitalised on the powerful running skills of Gareth Thomas, whose burst opened the way for first Martyn Williams and then Kevin Morgan to play in the winger.

The game naturally slowed as the Italians attempted to disrupt the play and catch their breath, and only a Rob Sidoli try against the country of his father's birth in the 73rd minute added to the Wales total.

The hosts hadn't enjoyed the best of luck, and were forced to replace some of their major talents at regular intervals; Mauro Bergamasco departed in the first half with a broken cheekbone, and goalkicker Roland de Marigny injured a knee in the second. But it was the effort expended in their opening game that was the principal reason for their failure to halt Wales' free-running rugby. As willing as they were, they couldn't live with the high-tempo and new-found belief of the best-balanced backline in the northern hemisphere, and a 30-point margin was as much as the Italians deserved.

As for Wales, it was an important win; not so much in the tally of points, but the manner with which they brutally exposed the opposition's weaknesses to secure the points. It signalled a ruthlessness and efficiency long lacking in the red ranks, and gave a profound indication that Ruddock's men were living up to the gathering hype.

Left: Hal Luscombe offloads. Following page: Shane Williams and Gareth Thomas feel the moment

ITALY		WALES	
Roland de Marigny	15	Gareth Thomas (c)	
Mirco Bergamasco	14	Hal Luscombe	
Walter Pozzebon	13	Tom Shanklin	
Andrea Masi	12	Gavin Henson	
Ludovico Nitoglia	11	Shane Williams	
Luciano Orquera	10	Stephen Jones	
Alessandro Troncon	9	Dwayne Peel	
Andrea Lo Cicero	1	Gethin Jenkins	
Fabio Ongaro	2	Mefin Davies	
Castrogiovanni	3	Adam Jones	
Santiago Dellape	4	Brent Cockbain	
Marco Bortolami (c)	5	Robert Sidoli	
Aaron Persico	6	Jonathan Thomas	
Mauro Bergamasco	7	Martyn Williams	
Sergio Parisse	8	Michael Owen	

Replacements: David Dal Maso for Mauro Bergamasco (23), Kaine Robertson for Pozzebon (54), Paul Griffen for Troncon (57), Salvatore Perugini for Castrogiovanni (58), Carlo Del Fava for Dellape (58), Giorgio Intoppa for Ongaro (68), Matteo Barbini for de Marigny (74)
Try: Orquera
Pen: de Marigny

Replacements: Kevin Morgan for Luscombe (54), Gareth Cooper for Peel (57), Ceri Sweeney for S Jones (61), Robin McBryde for Davies (62), John Yapp for A Jones (62), Ian Gough for Cockbain (62), Robin Sowden-Taylor for M Williams (75)
Tries: J Thomas, Shanklin, M Williams, Cockbain, S Williams, Sidoli
Cons: S Jones 4

Referee: Andrew Cole (Australia)

MATCH STATISTICS

Italy		Wales
7	Scrums Won	9
0	Scrums Lost	0
5	Penalties Conceded	8
79	Tackles Made	71
14	Missed Tackles	8
84	% Tackles Completed	89
28	Errors Made	27
4	Turn Overs Won	10
97	Passes Completed	136
28	Possessions Kicked	34
22	% Possessions Kicked	20
6	Poss. Kicked To Touch	10

RBS Man of the Match: Martyn Williams
Fresh from winning his 50th cap against England, Martyn Williams followed it up with a barnstorming display against the Azzurri. Showing off his full range of skills, he tackled ferociously and provided an openside masterclass in linking the rampant pack with the fleet-footed backs. He also scored what was probably the decisive try of the game before half-time; taking a pass from Hal Luscombe and avoiding the last ditch Italian defence to ground the ball on the upright of the post. Awesome!

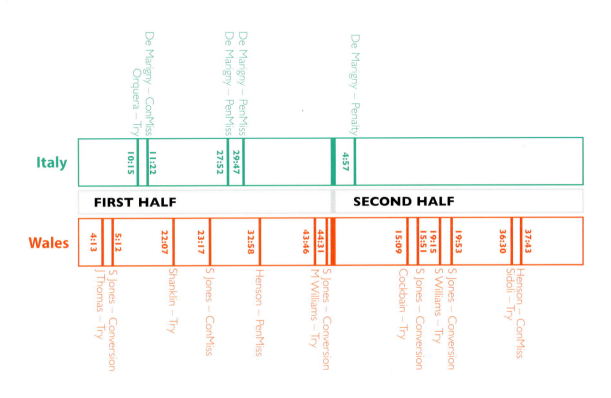

France 18 Wales 24

Stade de France

Saturday, February 26, 2005

Attendance: 78,250

FRANCE v WALES

Previous page: Dwayne Peel releases the ball. Left: Robert Sidoli climbs the highest. Right: Martyn Williams leads the victory cheers

Perhaps more than any other match in the Six Nations, the scintillating win over France at a boisterous, emotional Stade de France signalled the re-emergence of Wales as a genuine international force. After the fractious, nail-biting victory over England and the perfunctory dismissal of the Italians, the sensational second-half display to overturn a 15-6 half-time deficit in France's backyard transformed Wales from spirited contenders into the aristocrats of the tournament – with Scotland and Ireland to come, the vaunted Grand Slam was within Mike Ruddock's reach.

Not that the first 12 minutes offered much encouragement to the travelling legions that history was in the making. In sub-zero temperatures, France warmed-up quickest and opened the game with a point every 60 seconds, notching up tries from scrum-half Dimitri Yachvili and then Aurélien Rougerie, who used his 6ft 4in, 15st 7lb frame to ride roughshod over Shane Williams after a suspect trip on Gavin Henson by Serge Betsen had left the Welsh midfield exposed. The French were quite simply breathtaking, recycling with fluidity and purpose and constantly finding holes around the fringes of rucks that barely had time to form. The sterility of the games against Scotland and England, much lamented by the French press and bemoaned by the fickle Stade de France crowd, had been banished in a flurry of free-running exuberance that recalled the halcyon days of Blanco, Sella and Lagisquet.

Wales, however, remained in contention through a combination of tenacious defence, French indecision and a brace of penalty goals from Stephen Jones. The nine-point gap at the interval was hardly the unbridgeable gulf it had threatened to be in the opening quarter, though a cruel thumb injury to Gareth Thomas meant that Wales would be without their captain for

> *Exhaustion, pride, camaraderie ... you name it, I felt it*
> *Stephen Jones*

> *In modern rugby, it's never over unless you think it is*
> *Mike Ruddock*

> *To beat a top-five side away is massive. In that seven minutes of injury time, the spirit of this team shone through*
> *Martyn Williams*

> *No praise can be high enough for the current Wales team after pulling off one of the truly memorable results in the history of our country's rugby*
> *Barry John*

FRANCE v WALES

the second half. Within the first five minutes of the restart, Martyn Williams, already vying for player of the tournament, had touched down twice to hand the visitors a three-point lead. The first was sparked by some suitably dazzling handling from Henson, whose deft flick sent Stephen Jones on a jinking, 60-metre run upfield. The ball was quickly recycled and spread wide, where Shane Williams showed a clean pair of heels to his first-half tormentor Rougerie and delivered a perfectly executed inside pass to namesake Martyn for a simple finish. Before the French had settled themselves, Martyn Williams went over for his second. Spying a poorly organised defence at a penalty on their own line, he barged past Fabien Pelous and twisted to ground the ball just over the line.

It was breathtaking stuff. But just as the rampant Welsh looked like adding to their haul, new arrival Fréderic Michalak dropped a goal on 65 minutes to tie the game at 18-18. Amid the tumult, Stephen Jones re-established Welsh supremacy with a penalty and then, with six minutes to go, a coolly delivered drop goal of his own. The margin forced the French to desperate raids on the Welsh line, but just as gaps began to emerge, so thunderous Welsh tackles slammed them shut. Gethin Jenkins, now at tighthead after an Adam Jones substitution, was heroic, as was stand-in skipper Michael Owen. The climax was a nerve-shredding series of half-breaks, scrambling tackles, and last-ditch interventions.

As the clock ticked past 80 minutes, with the Welsh pack on their own line, referee Paul Honiss signalled that the next time the ball went dead, the final whistle would sound. Stephen Jones collected in his own in-goal area, turned to the stands behind him and hoofed the ball into the upper deck to seal one of the most memorable Welsh comebacks in recent memory. Despite the panic of 15,000 visiting fans, Jones knew exactly what he was doing. And in the circumstances, who was to argue?

Left: Stephen Jones' boot kept Wales in the hunt. Following page: "Alfie's" expression says it all

France		Wales
Julien Laharrague	15	Gareth Thomas (c)
Aurelien Rougerie	14	Kevin Morgan
Yannick Jauzion	13	Tom Shanklin
Damien Traille	12	Gavin Henson
Christophe Dominici	11	Shane Williams
Yann Delaigue	10	Stephen Jones
Dimitri Yachvili	9	Dwayne Peel
Sylvain Marconnet	1	Gethin Jenkins
Sebastien Bruno	2	Mefin Davies
Nicholas Mas	3	Adam Jones
Fabien Pelous (c)	4	Brent Cockbain
Jerome Thion	5	Robert Sidoli
Serge Betsen	6	Ryan Jones
Yannick Nyanga	7	Martyn Williams
Julien Bonnaire	8	Michael Owen

Replacements: William Servat for Bruno (41), Jean-Philippe Grandclaude for Traille (46), Frederic Michalak for Delaigue (49), Olivier Milloud for Mas (49), Imanol Harinordoquy for Bonnaire (59), Gregory Lamboley for Thion (74)
Tries: Yachvili, Rougerie
Con: Yachvili
Pen: Yachvili
Drop Goals: Michalak

Replacements: Rhys Williams for Thomas (41), Ceri Sweeney for Morgan (53), Robin McBryde for Davies (64), Gareth Cooper for Peel (67), John Yapp for A Jones (67), Jonathan Thomas for R Jones (77)
Tries: M Williams 2
Con: S Jones
Pens: S Jones 3
Drop Goal: S Jones

Referee: Paul Honniss (New Zealand)

MATCH STATISTICS

France		Wales
12	Scrums Won	11
0	Scrums Lost	0
9	Penalties Conceded	5
75	Tackles Made	88
6	Missed Tackles	12
92	% Tackles Completed	88
31	Errors Made	26
8	Turn Overs Won	9
164	Passes Completed	112
22	Possessions Kicked	30
11	% Possessions Kicked	21
10	Poss. Kicked To Touch	11

RBS Man of the Match: Stephen Jones

A commanding display of composure and courage under fire, this was one of Stephen Jones' finest showings in the red jersey. Blocking out the boos of the home support, Jones slotted home a 40-metre penalty to open the Welsh account and ended an embattled first half with another sweetly struck kick to keep his side in the chase. His bold break at the start of the second half led to the first of Martyn Williams' tries, which Jones converted. He revelled in reminding Fréderic Michalak that he wasn't the only class fly-half playing his rugby in France with a third penalty and a drop goal, the latter following some sublime approach work. At the death, it was fitting that Jones launched the ball over his own deadball line to end the game and seal the win.

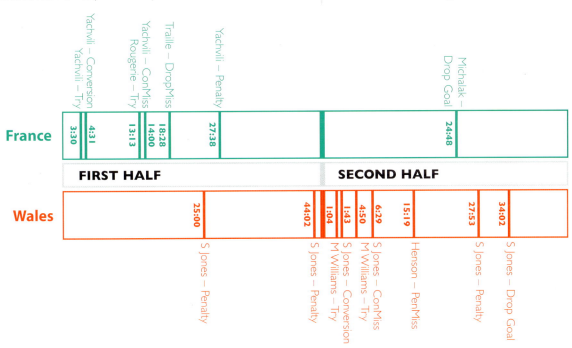

Scotland 22 Wales 46

Murrayfield

Sunday, March 13, 2005

Attendance: 63,430

SCOTLAND v WALES

Previous page: Dwayne Peel takes flight. Left: Ryan Jones gets his head down. Right: Martyn Williams puts in another tackle

It took approximately 140 seconds for Mike Ruddock's team to underline that this Wales XV suffers little in the way of stage fright. Taking advantage of a loose kick, blind-side flanker Ryan Jones put his scrum-capped head down, charged at Scottish forwards Scott Murray and Stuart Grimes and emerged practically untouched with an empty field in front of him. He received support from Rhys Williams, Martyn Williams and Gethin Jenkins, and gratefully accepted the return pass to flop over the line for a stunning opening salvo. With Wales just two games away from a first Grand Slam in a generation, the side could be forgiven for a few nervous moments, especially as Scotland had little but Celtic pride to play for. It is typical of this group of players, though, that anxiety is something they create in others, not what they experience themselves. Ryan Jones's bullocking run typified this new approach.

As if that start wasn't horrific enough for the Murrayfield crowd, they might have been tempted to retreat to the hospitality areas five minutes later. With the Scotland forwards punching holes in the Welsh line, an equalising try was imminent as Dan Parks sought to exploit a massive overlap – but instead of finding the arms of Chris Paterson, the ball sailed straight to the only red shirt in sight. The Scottish players stood aghast as Rhys Williams gleefully galloped 70 metres to double the advantage. And it only got better for the visitors. Less than five minutes later, Stephen Jones broke into midfield and fed skipper Michael Owen, who had to do nothing more than pop the ball to Shane Williams to complete the score. With just 14 minutes gone, the score was a scarcely credible 21-0.

After an exchange of penalty goals, with Scotland finally getting on the board after 23 minutes, Kevin Morgan made his first contribution with a simple finish after Tom

61

SCOTLAND v WALES

> We have not won anything yet, but we have shown that we are a good team. It's going to be a crazy week. It's going to be something special
> *Stephen Jones*

> They're the best side we've played. They'll be very hard to stop
> *Matt Williams, Scotland coach*

> The players are a credit to our nation. They have played with confidence, belief and ability
> *Mike Ruddock*

> We proved against France that we have the fitness and the physique, while we showed today that we can start a match. If we put it all together, who knows what we will be capable of?
> *Ryan Jones*

Left: Tom Shanklin on the hoof. Following page: Dwayne Peel goes in hard

Shanklin had bisected the latest woeful Scottish challenges, this time from Sean Lamont and Parks. Morgan was on hand again in first-half injury time to cross, after Dwayne Peel had expertly spotted a gap from the base of a retreating scrum. When the whistle sounded, the Welsh team were able to saunter down the tunnel with 38 points in the bag, and a gulf of 35 to play with for the remaining 40 minutes.

Unfortunately for the beleaguered Scots, the second half began in a similar vein to the first. On 49 minutes, Peel's presence of mind was again to the fore as he tapped a quick penalty and sent over Rhys Williams in the right-hand corner. Inevitably, Wales eased off the gas a little with the game won, and on 54 minutes, after gutsy work from Gordon Ross, Mike Blair set up Andy Craig for the try. Following the sin-binning of Brent Cockbain, Rory Lamont was able to exploit space on the wing to scuttle over with 10 minutes remaining, and this was followed by a Chris Paterson score after a thrilling break from Rory's brother, Sean. But Wales had the final word, with a Stephen Jones penalty completed the scoring.

Despite the margin of victory, and the fact that the game was essentially over as early as the 29th minute, there were those who were pointing to Scotland's late flurry as a sign that the Welsh juggernaut was not as unstoppable as it might seem. Ireland would gain heart from that, it was suggested. Of course, more learned observers noted that scoring a few tries when you're 35 points behind is, largely, an irrelevance, and the exhilarating rugby that opened up that gap should be the game's sole talking point. Inside 40 minutes, Michael Owen's men had scored more points against Scotland than any other Welsh side in Championship history. Few statistics could rival that.

Scotland		Wales
Chris Paterson	15	Kevin Morgan
Rory Lamont	14	Rhys Williams
Andy Craig	13	Tom Shanklin
Hugo Southwell	12	Gavin Henson
Sean Lamont	11	Shane Williams
Dan Parks	10	Stephen Jones
Chris Cusiter	9	Dwayne Peel
Tom Smith	1	Gethin Jenkins
Gordon Bulloch (c)	2	Mefin Davies
Gavin Kerr	3	Adam Jones
Stuart Grimes	4	Brent Cockbain
Scott Murray	5	Robert Sidoli
Simon Taylor	6	Ryan Jones
Jon Petrie	7	Martyn Williams
Allister Hogg	8	Michael Owen (c)

Replacements: Gordon Ross for Parks (41), Bruce Douglas for Kerr (41), Nathan Hines for Grimes (41), Mike Blair for Cusiter (44), Andrew Henderson for Craig (76)
Tries: Craig, R Lamont, Paterson
Cons: Paterson 2
Pen: Paterson

Replacements: Robin McBryde for Davies (50), Robin McBryde for Davies (50), John Yapp for A Jones (63), Hal Luscombe for R Williams (68), Jonathan Thomas for Cockbain (71), Ceri Sweeney for Henson (76)
Sin Bin: Cockbain (61)
Tries: R Jones, R Williams 2, S Williams, Morgan 2
Cons: S Jones 5
Pens: S Jones 2

Referee: Jonathan Kaplan (South Africa)

MATCH STATISTICS

Scotland		Wales
14	Scrums Won	9
0	Scrums Lost	0
8	Penalties Conceded	10
122	Tackles Made	160
14	Missed Tackles	25
89	% Tackles Completed	86
22	Errors Made	24
9	Turn Overs Won	10
214	Passes Completed	201
19	Possessions Kicked	17
8	% Possessions Kicked	7
10	Poss. Kicked To Touch	7

RBS Man of the Match: Dwayne Peel
Dwayne Peel was at his energetic best in Murrayfield, constantly prying and probing to look for gaps and trying to release his backs. He gave Lions rival Chris Cusiter a torrid time. He set up two tries; wriggling out of a tackle to release Kevin Morgan, and in the second half, spotting Scotland with their backs turned, he spun a 30-metre pass out to Rhys Williams to scamper over and put the game beyond Scotland. This typified Peel's impudence and opportunism – exemplifying a player at the top of his game.

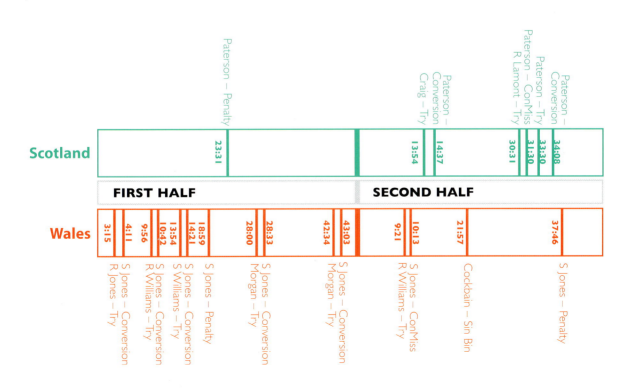

Wales 32 Ireland 20

Millennium Stadium

Saturday, March 19, 2005

Attendance: 74,500

Previous page: The dream is realised. Left: Tom Shanklin on the break. Right: Vocal threesome Charlotte Church, Max Boyce and Katherine Jenkins

March 19th, 2005 will be etched into the annals of Welsh sporting history as the day Wales secured a truly momentous first Grand Slam in 27 years. They defeated Ireland 32-20 to set off extraordinary scenes inside the Millennium Stadium.

The pre-match hyperbole had been all about Wales and the Grand Slam. Ireland on the other hand, had been dealt a hammer blow by France the week earlier – seeing their first Grand Slam since 1948 vanish with the smiling Christophe Dominici. Eddie O'Sullivan knew then it would be a big ask to raise the side's morale. And so it proved.

Prior to the game, the streets of Cardiff had taken on a carnival atmosphere, with up to 15,000 fans gathering outside the City Hall to watch the match on a big screen. Inside the Millennium Stadium, the vocal Irish support, fresh from their St Patrick's Day and Cheltenham Gold Cup excesses, were simply overwhelmed by the fervent Welsh support. The ante was upped further when Katherine Jenkins, Charlotte Church and the old stager Max Boyce belted out *Hen Wlad Fy Nhadau* only to be engulfed by one of the most patriotic National Anthems ever heard in the stadium. By the time Wynne Evans swaggered towards the half-way line singing *Bread of Heaven*, it would have taken an iron-willed Irishman not to fear for the men in green. Momentum was on Wales' side. The biggest surprise for those fans taking their seats was that speedster Rhys Williams had a groin strain and was being replaced by ageing warhorse, and centre, Mark Taylor.

The game started quietly enough with Ronan O'Gara settling the Irish nerves by opening the scoring. But any thoughts that this would be a Celtic love-in were dispelled when Irish captain O'Driscoll raked Tom Shanklin illegally, giving away a penalty in the process. Wales levelled after 12 minutes thanks to a drop goal by the silver boot of

69

WALES v IRELAND

> *We put our bodies on the line and to hear that final whistle was pure joy*
> **Michael Owen**

> *We've had to live through bad days, we've been shot down and written off, but we've come through. To do this you have to be a team, you have to care for it in a deep way*
> **Gareth Thomas**

> *Once I'd charged it down, it was a case of 'hold on'. It was uncharted territory for me*
> **Gethin Jenkins**

> *The fans have been awesome, they've followed us everywhere and this is a great reward for them*
> **Dwayne Peel**

Gavin Henson. However, it wasn't until the 16th minute that the blue touch paper was lit after an O'Gara clearance was charged down by Gethin Jenkins. Jenkins showed remarkable pace for a big man, and no little footballing skills to hack ahead and touch down for the game's first try. After Stephen Jones converted, Wales went into a 10-3 lead. The lead was added to by a mammoth 52-metre penalty from Henson and a penalty kick from Jones, that was cancelled out by O'Gara. 16-6 up at half-time, Wales were cheered into their dressing room. The Grand Slam was only 40 minutes away.

The second half started off as the first had ended – with Wales in the ascendancy. Stephen Jones added two more penalties after some concerted Welsh pressure, before Wales applied the *coup de grâce* with a sparkling try from comeback kid Kevin Morgan, after Tom Shanklin had cut the Irish midfield in two, following some early good work from Michael Owen. Wales continued to ask questions of the Irish defence with Shane Williams and Dwayne Peel's counter-attacking causing problems and Gethin Jenkins' crunching tackling – notably on Reggie Corrigan – keeping the Irish attacks at bay. With Wales 29-6 up and coasting, the Irish came back into the game; replacement David Humphreys allowing Ireland to throw off their conservative shackles and start playing a more expansive game. Their reward came in the 66th minute with a try from prop Marcus Horan. More pressure from the Irish meant they scored another try in the 76th minute through Geordan Murphy to bring the scores to 32-20. A few Welsh fans may have shifted uneasily in their seats for the last few minutes but with the final whistle came a triumphant roar loud enough to exercise 27 years of hurt.

Left: Shane Williams looking to counter-attack. Following page: Grand Slam heroes

WALES		IRELAND
Kevin Morgan	15	Geordan Murphy
Mark Taylor	14	Girvan Dempsey
Tom Shanklin	13	Brian O'Driscoll (c)
Gavin Henson	12	Kevin Maggs
Shane Williams	11	Denis Hickie
Stephen Jones	10	Ronan O'Gara
Dwayne Peel	9	Peter Stringer
Gethin Jenkins	1	Reggie Corrigan
Mefin Davies	2	Shane Byrne,
Adam Jones	3	John Hayes
Brent Cockbain	4	Malcolm O'Kelly
Rob Sidoli	5	Paul O'Connell
Ryan Jones	6	Simon Easterby
Martyn Williams	7	Johnny O'Connor
Michael Owen (c)	8	Anthony Foley

Replacements: John Yapp for A Jones (67), Robin McBryde for Davies (69)
Tries: Jenkins, Morgan
Cons: S Jones 2
Pens: Henson, S Jones 4
Drop Goal: Henson

Replacements: David Humphreys for O'Gara (51), Marcus Horan for Corrigan (59), Frankie Sheahan for Byrne (63), Donncha O'Callaghan for O'Kelly (63), Eric Miller for Foley (59)
Tries: Horan, Murphy
Cons: Humphreys 2
Pens: O'Gara 2

Referee: Chris White (England)

MATCH STATISTICS

Wales		Ireland
9	Scrums Won	11
0	Scrums Lost	1
10	Penalties Conceded	11
91	Tackles Made	57
9	Missed Tackles	7
91	% Tackles Completed	89
19	Errors Made	21
10	Turn Overs Won	2
84	Passes Completed	109
27	Possessions Kicked	22
24	% Possessions Kicked	16
9	Poss. Kicked To Touch	8

RBS Man of the Match: Dwayne Peel

Dwayne Peel further enhanced his burgeoning reputation with a second successive man-of-the-match display, showing a cool head throughout. Small in stature but big on presence he was a hive of activity at every breakdown. He was simply electric around the fringes, using quick tap penalties throughout the game to keep Ireland on the back foot. Looking a Lion to his bootlaces he outpaced and out-thought the more experienced Peter Stringer from start to finish.

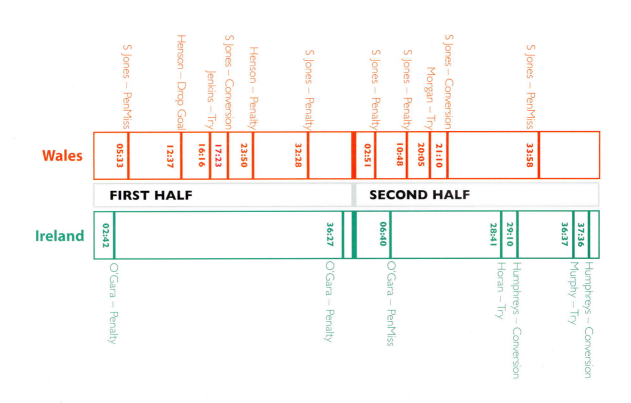

Joyful and triumphant

Five games, 26 players and a nation that never lost faith. Here, some of those fans bear witness to their own personal Grand Slam pilgrimages

The historic Grand Slam of 2005 was testament to the hard work and diligence of Mike Ruddock and his record-breaking squad. However, none of the aforementioned players and management take full credit for their success. To a man, they have all spoken of the huge lift given to them by the fans that followed them all over Europe, supporting and bolstering their heroes. The team have applauded the Welsh fans as the best in world rugby and integral to their success; lifting them in times of strife.

Take the first game in Cardiff. When Wales were staring at a cruel defeat, they sensed that one man, Gavin Henson, had a date with destiny and chanted his name to take that winning kick. In Paris, when Wales faced yet more insurmountable odds – 15-6 down at half-time and backs to the walls in the last quarter – they were thankful for 15,000 patriotic fans bellowing *Bread of Heaven* into the cold winter's evening, inspiring them to more feats of herculean endeavour. Think of the joy on the faces of the fans in Rome, where Wales' gladiatorial charges put the Italians to the sword with ruthless efficiency. Or of Edinburgh, where Scotland's capital was engulfed in a red wave early in March, when a rumoured 40,000 fans besieged planes, trains, buses and cars to scramble up to Murrayfield to behold one of the finest performances by a Welsh side in decades. The fans saved their best till last in their spiritual home, where, pre-match, even the Irish players admitted to sensing a "special atmosphere" as 200,000 Welsh supporters, from all over the world, let alone every corner of Wales, descended on Cardiff for the finale. The atmosphere in the stadium will live long in the memory and for those lucky enough join in with Max, Charlotte and Katherine, they can forever say, "I was there".

The following pages pay tribute to those fans, with a few personal insights into a never-to-be-forgotten tournament.

WALES v ENGLAND
GORDON WILKINS, WHITCHURCH

Being an ardent Welsh rugby supporter all my life, I was looking forward to the first match of the season; the big one – Wales against England. There was an air of expectation among every Welshman in the land. Wales had not beaten England in Cardiff since 1993, when Ieuan Evans sauntered past Rory Underwood to score that famous try at the old Cardiff Arms Park.

The day started at Llandaff North Rugby club where the atmosphere was buzzing, though the tension built in the packed club house as the game drew nearer.

As the landlord of The Plough in Whitchurch, all the conversations I have had over the bar in the previous weeks had been about the game. I knew we

were capable, especially with injuries to the Chariot. England were there for the taking, and we knew it.

We headed over to the Millennium Stadium, where no one could have prepared me for the sight that greeted me. St Mary's Street was a sea of red. Flags were flying, Welshmen were singing away with pints in their hands – there were even babies with dragons painted on their faces!

I had a sneaking suspicion the English fans were a little too confident that "Team England" would roll over the Welsh Dragon – how wrong they were! The game was over in what seemed like minutes; Shane Williams scored that brilliant first try, Grewcock should have walked – permanently for that kick on little Dwayne – and then Henson, what can I say? The kick was magnificent. The rest, as they say, is history.

As I headed back to the pub, the atmosphere was still there. A few more Welsh fans seemed to have done their fair share of "celebrating", but I had no voice left to call last orders. What a day!

ITALY v WALES
SHAUN HARDING, TONYREFAIL (left)

What makes the Rome trip special? It starts with the taxi ride into the Eternal City. Picture the chariot race in *Ben Hur* and you're halfway to experiencing Roman drivers. The white-knuckle thrill of the stampede into the city is then replaced by the magic of the Trevi Fountain after dark. Gypsies selling roses compete for attention with kilt-wearing Osprey supporters from Llansamlet.

Then comes match day and the realisation that, last night, four Strongbows cost £28 in one of the Irish pubs. On the walk to the ground we stumble across the magnificent monument to Vittorio Emanuele II and increase the profits of a small café near the Spanish Steps. Welsh fans appear out of every street and alley. Refreshments are taken in the Piazza del Popolo before the final push to reach the ground. *Calon Lan* rings out across the Piazza as Italian TV crews film the invasion. Another invasion takes place in the café as the cleaner is surrounded by Welsh men and women queuing to use her toilet.

Finally the game. There's fantastic singing to cheer on the boys and just when you think there are no Italians in the crowd a huge roar goes up as Italy win the toss.

The Italy trip is *the Beatles* playing in the Cavern, it's America before the white man, it's that magic place you keep a secret for as long as you can!

FRANCE v WALES
PAUL WALLEK, PARIS (right)

There was a sense that something was beginning to stir by the time of the Paris game. On arriving at the Stade de France an hour before kick-off, the road to the stadium was awash with red, with barely a tinge of blue in sight – expectations were running amok! A couple of beers outside with my French friend Xavier only fed the anticipation, but after entering the stadium I found that the Welsh support was at either end of the stadium and in the upper reaches of the vast stands, while I was sat among a pack of French corporate bankers; me complete with red shirt and hat, my French friend complete with blue shirt and tricolore hat.

The feeling of being on the outside was reinforced with the first passages of play; the French annihilated us. Behind me, my three new friends from south west France (average age 65) were cheering away and telling me (I think) that it was all over. Half-time came as a welcome relief. After a four quid, non-alcoholic beer (zut alors!), Xavier suggested we swap hats as a sign of solidarity. Maybe that was what did it. Martyn Williams single-handedly dragged us into the lead and we never looked back.

My three OAPs insisted Xavier and I swap back our hats, but the damage was already done. The ends of the stadium were singing raucously where previously they had sat in quiet desperation. I left with a huge smile, as did all the Welsh support, while most of the French were saying, "better to you than the English." I couldn't agree more.

SCOTLAND v WALES
SCOTT EUDEN, CANTON (centre)

Edinburgh here we come! With the England and Italy games behind us and the second-half performance against France fresh in our minds, the good-humoured conversation among the thousands of Welsh supporters on the long walk to Murrayfield was filled with confidence.

The atmosphere was electric, with a blanket of red filling the stadium. A lone piper on the stadium roof and a rousing rendition of *Flower of Scotland* did their best to inspire the Scots, but it just added to the adrenalin.

Sat behind the posts, the try blitz happened right under our noses, and we found ourselves 21-0 up after just 15 minutes. We hardly had time to sit down and swig from our hip flask of Cognac before we were up off our seats to celebrate more points, to chants of "It's just like watching Brazil"!

The ball handling was a joy to watch and the lads on the field seemed to be enjoying themselves almost as much as the fans – even the Scottish supporters were applauding the Welsh play. We sat beside two hilarious Welsh supporters dressed as Batman and Robin. They must have been 70 years old; beer bellies squeezed into lycra and spectacles over their face masks. Legendary!

At 38-3, the second half was a bit of an anti-climax. Wales appeared to be conserving their energy for Ireland, but credit to Scotland, they worked hard to pull back a few tries. At the final whistle fans started talking about the Grand Slam; but that could wait until next week – we had some serious celebrating to do in the Grass Market. So many Welsh fans, so many pubs and so much singing! On the long train journey back to Cardiff, not many words were exchanged. We all looked and felt like hell, but each one of us carried a smile. Thank you Edinburgh!

WALES v IRELAND

GARETH REESE, BRIDGEND (below left)

"They roll it back when Wales attack, so God can watch us play!" Max Boyce re-inventing his anthem of '70s rugby glory seemed so apt at the start of this clash of the Celtic titans. Wales had cut a swathe through international rugby since their so-near-but-so-far defeat at the hands of the All Blacks back in November. No-one could have anticipated the way in which they surged to glory with such style prior to this final winner-takes-all epic.

With an Irish wife and two friends staying from Wicklow, I was in the minority that St Paddy's weekend, until I boarded the train at Bridgend, jam-packed with fervent Grand Slam believers from all points west. The craic was mighty and Cardiff was an incredible ocean of red and green. Hundreds queued for the pubs in the spring sunshine as we made our way to meet up with friends at City Hall. Confronted by a horde of thousands, we quickly turned tail, desperate to find our first pint of the afternoon. At the Hilton a throng of green-clad fans armed with

camera-phones let out a huge roar as the Irish team were ushered onto their bus.

The game was mesmeric. After a quiet opening 10 minutes, Wales displayed all that we desired, from the Henson drop-goal to the Kevin Morgan try – the icing on the Grand Slam cake. As we all counted down the final 10 seconds and the cheer went up, not a soul moved. No clamour for the exits, no rush for the bar; Welsh and Irish stood together to savour an unforgettable moment. My father was there in 1978 against France, I'm glad to be able to say that "I was there" too!

Words of wisdom

All through the Grand Slam campaign, the world's greatest rugby player, **Gareth Edwards**, kept the readers of the *Western Mail* up to date with his views through his exclusive weekly column. Here we chart the thoughts, predictions and reactions of the man who played in three Grand Slam winning teams in the '70s

WALES v ENGLAND

BEFORE

"It's time for Gavin Henson to put his money where his mouth is. The Ospreys centre has the talent and the confidence to be one of the best rugby players in the world"

"This Wales team has everything it takes to be one of the great sides – except consistency. And they can put that crucial factor into their armoury if they reproduce the high-intensity 80-minute performance we saw against New Zealand"

"This is going to be a close game and Wales need to avoid mistakes if they're to finish on top. My message to the team: Just do it lads"

AFTER

"Make no mistake – that was one of the most important wins in our rugby history. If the thrilling victory over England hasn't given them confidence, nothing will"

"Saturday's Test was always going to be a watershed match, and I think things will really kick off for this side now. The final Six Nations match against Ireland could decide the Triple Crown, the Championship title, or even the Grand Slam"

"It wasn't a great performance but it was a great win. If they can play badly and beat the world champions, what's going to happen when they play well?"

ITALY v WALES

BEFORE

"We've got to play the game at our pace, impose our own authority on the 80 minutes. That means being quick to the breakdown, getting turnovers and making good ball available to unleash our excellent back division"

"[Wales] have far too much firepower for the Italians. Play the game the traditional old Welsh way and, by 3pm, I'm convinced we will be celebrating another Wales win"

AFTER

"Six tries in an away game in what is proving to be arguably the tightest Six Nations Championship of all time tells its own story"

"Each game under Mike Ruddock has revealed something new about his Welsh team"

"Let's not forget that while we have won back-to-back Championship victories for the first time since 1994, we still haven't won a Triple Crown since 1988 or a Grand Slam since 1978. It is all out there for this team to win"

FRANCE v WALES

BEFORE

"Brutal, abrasive, uncompromising and, at times, frightening. Welcome to Paris!"

"In Paris, they will quickly learn, you have to scrap for every point. Wales have to meet fire with fire. Any sign of turning the other cheek will be interpreted as Welsh weakness"

"In the old days, whoever won between Wales and France would go on to win either the Grand Slam or the title. Let's hope there is an omen there"

AFTER

"What a team this is in the making. They might not be the finished article yet, or have that Grand Slam in their locker, but it surely can't be far off"

"The new spirit among this exciting and determined group of players came shining to the fore. They took it on the chin, sucked up some air and fought back magnificently"

"If the win over England was a turning point, then turning this game around so brilliantly in the second half could be the making of this team"

SCOTLAND v WALES

BEFORE

"To hope Scotland don't 'turn up' at Murrayfield is like hoping the sun doesn't come up in the morning. When the bagpipes start playing, Scotland start playing. It's as simple as that"

"The first 20 minutes will be played at a heck of a pace, but that should suit Wales. If we nail them early, we'll run away with it"

AFTER

"The way that Michael Owen and his side played is the true Welsh way. It was breathtaking, spell-binding, fantastic to watch. You could hardly find enough superlatives with which to praise the attitude and application of every player in red in those magical opening minutes"

"I cannot remember either playing in or seeing a better half of rugby by a Welsh side in my lifetime than we all marvelled at in Edinburgh"

"They have grown individually and collectively"

WALES v IRELAND

BEFORE

"How on Earth have we come this far in such a short space of time? Part of me is still shuddering from the Six Nations whitewash two seasons ago"

"The promise of the November performances has been turned into concrete evidence that we are not a nation of chokers"

"It is going to be a special occasion – a potential career changing one for the players. I can't pick a winner, but I have enough confidence in the way this Welsh side has performed to realise they have the ability and desire to win"

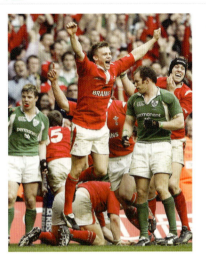

AFTER

"Welsh rugby has a new set of icons. We've finally put to bed the bad days of the past 27 years and given ourselves something to be proud about"

"The events of Saturday, 19 March, 2005 will go into Welsh history. Not just the epic performance on the field of play, but the way in which this group of players encouraged a whole nation to express itself"

Copy courtesy of the Western Mail.

Statistics

Final standings

TEAM	P	W	D	L	F	A	PD	PTS
Wales	5	5	0	0	151	77	74	10
France	5	4	0	1	134	82	52	8
Ireland	5	3	0	2	126	101	25	6
England	5	2	0	3	121	77	44	4
Scotland	5	1	0	4	84	155	-71	2
Italy	5	0	0	5	55	179	-124	0

Top five...

POINTS SCORERS		TRY SCORERS		GOAL SCORERS	
Ronan O'Gara (Ire)	60	Mark Cueto (Eng)	4	Stephen Jones (Wal)	22
Stephen Jones (Wal)	57	Kevin Morgan (Wal)	3	Ronan O'Gara (Ire)	20
Dimitri Yachvili (Fra)	53	Jamie Noon (Eng)	3	Dimitri Yachvili (Fra)	18
Chris Paterson (Sco)	49	Martyn Williams (Wal)	3	Chris Paterson (Sco)	16
Charlie Hodgson (Eng)	39	Shane Williams (Wal)	3	Charlie Hodgson (Eng)	15

Team performances

SCRUMS WON – LOST		LINEOUTS WON – LOST		TURNOVERS WON	
Scotland	56 – 1	England	90 – 12	Wales	45
Wales	45 – 1	Ireland	83 – 10	England	40
England	40 – 0	Italy	82 – 16	France	40
France	38 – 0	Scotland	72 – 13	Scotland	38
Italy	36 – 2	France	86 – 10	Italy	33
Ireland	31 – 1	Wales	73 – 16	Ireland	32

TACKLES MADE		MISSED TACKLES		TACKLES COMPLETED	
Wales	476	Italy	70	France	91%
Scotland	408	Wales	62	England	90%
France	399	Scotland	54	Ireland	90%
Italy	370	France	39	Wales	88%
Ireland	332	Ireland	37	Scotland	88%
England	301	England	32	Italy	84%

ERRORS MADE		PASSES COMPLETED		POSSESSION KICKED	
Wales	476	Scotland	763	Ireland	156
Scotland	408	England	756	Italy	156
France	399	Wales	632	Scotland	153
Italy	370	France	606	England	141
Ireland	332	Italy	506	Wales	137
England	301	Ireland	442	France	131

WALES
squad profiles
2004/05

Gareth Thomas

Club: Toulouse
Born: 25.07.74, Bridgend
Position: Full-back
Height: 1.88m
Weight: 103kg

Gareth Thomas' first season as captain of Wales was cut cruelly short in the throes of battle during France's first-half pummelling of the Welsh line. He'd been in inspired form until then, galvanising those around him with assured full-back play, breaks in the open and fierce defence. His copybook was somewhat blotted with a sin-binning against England for a retaliatory shove on Danny Grewcock after Dwayne Peel had received a boot to the head, but during the Italy game, Thomas cut loose constantly, making numerous breaks in open play. It was against France that, having withstood a fearsome Gallic onslaught, Thomas took a fall and broke his thumb in five places. Showing great character despite his personal disappointment, Thomas stayed with the squad for the rest of the campaign.

2005 RBS 6 Nations: England, Italy, France
Points: 0

Michael Owen

Club: Dragons
Born: 07.11.80, Pontypridd
Position: No 8
Height: 1.96m
Weight: 115kg

Michael Owen established himself as one of Wales' finest talents during the 2005 tournament. There was no better passer in the competition; whether it was cross-field torpedoes, cute offloads or long deliveries, Owen found his man. He set up tries for Shane Williams against England and Jonathan Thomas against Italy, and started off the move that led to Kevin Morgan's try against Ireland. His strong ball-handling, industry around the fringes and support play led to a Lions call up. Taking up the reins of captaincy from Gareth Thomas in the second half of the French game, Owen became Wales' 122nd captain by leading the team out for the first time against Scotland and against Ireland the following week; his diligent, cerebral leadership ensuring a measure of continuity for Wales' remaining games.

2005 RBS 6 Nations: England, Italy, France, Scotland, Ireland
Points: 0

Kevin Morgan

Club: Dragons
Born: 23.02.77, Cilfynydd
Position: Full-back
Height: 1.78m
Weight: 84kg

There can be few more heartening stories in Grand Slam year than that of Kevin Morgan. At the start of the season he was clubless, had been ravaged by injuries and hadn't played for Wales for over a year. With his free-scoring form for the Newport Gwent Dragons, he side-stepped his way into the Six Nations squad and then the starting line-up; first on the right wing against France and then as full-back cover for Gareth Thomas – scoring two tries in the 46-22 win over Scotland. He scored the decisive try in Wales' Grand Slam clincher against Ireland, running a brilliant support line from a Tom Shanklin pass. A natural full-back, Morgan's reading of the game and intuitive running angles made the captain's loss less telling.

2005 RBS 6 Nations: England (r), Italy (r), France, Scotland, Ireland
Points: 15 – 3T

Rhys Williams

Club: Blues
Born: 23.02.80, Cardiff
Position: Wing
Height: 1.78m
Weight: 88kg

Rhys Williams came late to the Grand Slam party, missing the England and Italy games due to thumb ligament damage. However, by the France game, Rhys was back on the bench and raring to go. His chance came. Taking to the field against the French following Gareth Thomas' broken thumb, Rhys kept the French defence on its toes throughout the second half. He was preferred to Hal Luscombe for the Scotland game and his selection was vindicated when he scored a brace; the first a 75-metre interception try, the second, a simple run in to the corner after some quick thinking by Dwayne Peel, extending his all-time Six Nations try total to nine. Unfortunately for Rhys, his luck ran out when he failed to shake off a calf strain before the Ireland game and was forced to pull out on the morning of the final clash.

2005 RBS 6 Nations: France (r), Scotland
Points: 10 – 2T

Tom Shanklin

Club: **Blues**
Born: **24.11.79, Harrow, England**
Position: **Centre**
Height: **1.88m**
Weight: **98kg**

On the fringes of the first-team at the outset of the 2005 Six Nations tournament, Tom Shanklin ended the campaign virtually irreplaceable. A starter in every match in his preferred outside-centre position, Shanks' tough-tackling, abrasive style and canny knack for scoring important tries have seen him catapulted into the Lions squad. He was many commentators' Man of the Match against Ireland, outplaying the talismanic O'Driscoll, and it was Shanklin who played the key role in the all-important Kevin Morgan score, taking route one to the line before a neat offload. He always managed to find space in the most congested of midfields with some great outside-centre play. Shanklin's intelligent distribution of the ball caused opposition defences more than a few headaches.

2005 RBS 6 Nations: England, Italy, France, Scotland, Ireland
Points: 5 – 1T

Shane Williams

Club: **Ospreys**
Born: **26.02.77, Swansea**
Position: **Wing**
Height: **1.71m**
Weight: **82kg**

Shane Williams is one of the undoubted stars of the Welsh team. A diminutive winger by today's standards, he champions nimble feet, speed of thought and a touch of old-fashioned guile. Shane cemented his reputation as a clinical finisher with three tries: touching down against England with the game's only score; versus Italy, where he finished off the try of the game after a Kevin Morgan offload; and Scotland, where he grounded a Stephen Jones-inspired move in the first-half. His darting runs in open play and electric bursts in tight situations mean that he can beat men one-on-one for fun, and with 24 tries in 29 appearances, he has one of the best strike rates in world rugby. He was Wales' joint-top try-scorer of the campaign with Kevin Morgan and Martyn Williams.

2005 RBS 6 Nations: England, Italy, France, Scotland, Ireland
Points: 15 – 3T

Gavin Henson

Club: **Ospreys**
Born: **01.02.82, Bridgend**
Position: **Centre**
Height: **1.83m**
Weight: **98kg**

The Six Nations Championship proved to be a springboard for Gavin Henson. From being a relative unknown outside the Principality before the competition, his impact in the England game, capped with a majestic, match-winning 44-metre penalty, was nothing short of sensational. He proved to be a fierce tackler and his dumping of debutant Mathew Tait in the same game has to be one of the defining moments of the tournament. He finished the campaign in style, courtesy of a drop goal via Reggie Corrigan's finger tips and an audacious 52-metre penalty to keep Wales in control. With a glorious range of kicking, sleight of hand, strong running lines and brutal tackling, Henson possesses a game with few weaknesses. He was a deserving Man of the Match against England.

2005 RBS 6 Nations: England, Italy, France, Scotland, Ireland
Points: 9 – 2P, 1DG

Stephen Jones

Club: **Clermont Auvergne**
Born: **08.12.77, Carmarthen**
Position: **Fly-half**
Height: **1.85m**
Weight: **94kg**

Stephen Jones enjoyed his finest Six Nations to date. Clearly a more rounded player thanks to his experience with Clermont Auvergne, Jones' influence was rewarded with the vice-captaincy for the decisive Ireland game. He collected a Man-of-the-Match award for his inspirational performance against France, the highlight of which was a jinking 60-metre dash upfield to set Martyn Williams' on the the comeback trail. His cool penalty and drop goal in the same game kept Wales' noses in front. Jones was also instrumental in Wales' thumping win over Scotland, consistently breaking the Scots defence. He is the second-highest points scorer in Welsh history, with 441 points in 47 Tests, and ended the Six Nation's campaign with 57 points, second only to Ronan O'Gara's tally of 60.

2005 RBS 6 Nations: England, Italy, France, Scotland, Ireland
Points: 57 – 12C, 10P, 1DG

Dwayne Peel

Club: Scarlets
Born: 31.08.81, Carmarthen
Position: Scrum-half
Height: 1.75m
Weight: 86kg

That Dwayne Peel managed to keep a player of Gareth Cooper's calibre on the bench for the duration of the 2005 Six Nations is testament to how highly regarded the young Wales scrum-half is. The 23-year-old had an impressive Championship, winning two Man-of-the-Match awards, against Scotland and Ireland respectively. Peel is a menace for opposing scrum-halves, his sniping runs around the base of the scrum and quick-tap penalties continually putting the opposition on the back foot. Against Scotland, it was his quick thinking that set up Rhys Williams for an audacious second-half score, and his dumping of Gordon Bulloch at the start of the game was an unequivocal statement of intent. His outstanding form led to a well deserved Lions call-up.

2005 RBS 6 Nations: England, Italy, France, Scotland, Ireland
Points: 0

Mefin Davies

Club: Gloucester
Born: 02.09.72, Nantgaredig
Position: Hooker
Height: 1.78m
Weight: 95kg

Mefin Davies was omnipresent throughout Wales' 2005 Six Nations campaign, managing to shake off a host of aches and pains to take part in all five games. He played with remarkable commitment, passion and no little skill to retain the hooker's birth, despite strong competition from Robin McBryde.
A combative extra flanker in the loose and skilled technician in the set-piece, Davies is seldom seen going backwards. He was Wales' first-choice hooker throughout the Championship and, indeed, for the previous three games as well – his longest run in the Welsh team to date. Mefin's unabated commitment to Wales over the past season, despite the offer of a lucrative contract by Stade Francais – the caveat being that he forfeited his Welsh career – was rewarded with a richly deserved Grand Slam.

2005 RBS 6 Nations: England, Italy, France, Scotland, Ireland
Points: 0

Gethin Jenkins

Club: Blues
Born: 17.11.80, Pontypridd
Position: Prop
Height: 1.88m
Weight: 121kg

Gethin Jenkins has rapidly become a talisman for the Welsh team; he was nothing short of a revelation in this Championship. Of his many attributes, it is his versatility in being able to make the short walk from loose head to tight head – a role he filled valiantly when holding steady in the light of a French bombardment in the final 10 minutes of the game at the Stade de France – that is so important. Jenkins is an asset in the loose, comfortable with the ball in hand and possessing genuine footballing skills. He has also proved a ferocious tackler, a fact Reggie Corrigan will attest to. His *coup de grâce* came against Ireland, where he was able to charge down a Ronan O'Gara clearance and hack the ball to the line to set Wales on their way to the Grand Slam, sealing his selection for the Lions Tour of New Zealand.

2005 RBS 6 Nations: England, Italy, France, Scotland, Ireland
Points: 5 – 1T

Adam Jones

Club: Ospreys
Born: 08.03.81, Swansea
Position: Prop
Height: 1.83m
Weight: 121kg

Adam Jones has continued to develop his game and is now widely recognised as a world-class prop. As an anchor to the hugely improved Welsh scrum, Jones was at the coalface throughout the 2005 Six Nations Championship. He also contributed in the loose, bullocking around the fringes and putting in some full-blooded hits. He started all of Wales' Six Nations games and has been integral to the side's strong scrummaging performances and set-pieces. While not one of the Welsh team's headline-grabbers, his strong defence and consistently impressive tackle count mean he is a vital cog in Mike Ruddock's revitalised pack. He has worked hard on his overall conditioning and is now a feared and respected opponent.

2005 RBS 6 Nations: England, Italy, France, Scotland, Ireland
Points: 0

Brent Cockbain

Club: Ospreys
Born: 15.11.74, Coffs Harbour, Australia
Position: Lock
Height: 2.04m
Weight: 119kg

One of Wales' most improved players of the 2005 campaign, Brent Cockbain had an outstanding Six Nations Championship, providing some much needed clout to the Welsh scrum. He used all of his massive six foot eight frame to disrupt opposition jumpers and was key in stabilising Wales' perennial achilles heel. A highlight of Cockbain's tournament was undoubtedly his debut international try against Italy. Taking the ball at pace from a pass from Jonathan Thomas 25 metres out, he swatted full-back Roland de Marigny with a powerful hand-off and galloped under the posts. Cockbain's assured, physical approach ensured that the pack were never outmuscled and he can be considered unfortunate to have missed out on a place in the Lions squad.

2005 RBS 6 Nations: England, Italy, France, Scotland, Ireland
Points: 5 – 1T

Ryan Jones

Club: Ospreys
Born: 13.03.81, Newport
Position: Flanker
Height: 1.96m
Weight: 112kg

Ryan Jones could stake a firm claim to being Wales' most improved player of the tournament. Jones overcame a nervous start to close the Six Nations as first-choice blindside. He was given his chance following an injury to Dafydd Jones, coming on as a replacement against England. He missed the Italy game through a shoulder injury but was given the nod for the last three games, his physical presence preferred to that of the more lightweight Jonathan Thomas. Jones saved his best performance for the Scots with a barnstorming show. He scored a fine debut try, bullocking through two Scottish tacklers to set up the move, and was Wales' top tackler in the game. Against Ireland he was a defensive rock in the latter stages, as the men in green applied pressure to the Welsh defence.

2005 RBS 6 Nations: England (r), France, Scotland, Ireland
Points: 5 – 1T

Robert Sidoli

Club: Blues
Born: 21.06.79, Merthyr
Position: Lock
Height: 1.99m
Weight: 115kg

A year ago, Robert Sidoli probably never dreamt that he'd be part of a victorious Grand Slam winning side. However, in spite of injuries and a temporary loss of form, he played his way back into the squad to become one of Wales' unsung heroes. He celebrated his return to the Welsh team with a thoroughly consistent Six Nations season, developing a close relationship with Brent Cockbain and winning his fair share of lineout ball, while spoiling plenty of opposition set-pieces. His prolific workrate and dogged driving around the fringes saw him performing heroically against France. Like Cockbain, he will have particularly fond memories of the Italy game, where he scored a debut try for his country, taking a pass from Ceri Sweeney to crash over the line.

2005 RBS 6 Nations: England, Italy, France, Scotland, Ireland
Points: 5 – 1T

Martyn Williams

Club: Blues
Born: 01.09.75, Pontypridd
Position: Flanker
Height: 1.83m
Weight: 99kg

Martyn Williams was the form openside flanker in this Six Nations tournament. After making a speedy recovery from a neck injury, he won his 50th cap in the game against England. He received the Man-of-the-Match award against Italy, using his nous and experience to ground a ball on the post when he was hauled down short of the line. He was an inspiration in the France match, finishing off a brace of tries in four minutes to cap a remarkable Welsh second-half comeback. Williams gave a masterclass in openside play, spoiling and linking forwards and backs seamlessly, and coming out as the top tackler in the competition with 57 in total. He was voted Six Nations Man of the Championship and has been called up to the Lions for a second time.

2005 RBS 6 Nations: England, Italy, France, Scotland, Ireland
Points: 15 – 3T

Robin McBryde

Club: Scarlets
Born: 03.07.70, Bangor
Position: Hooker
Height: 1.80m
Weight: 108kg

Robin McBryde recovered from a long-standing neck problem to feature as a replacement in four of this year's Six Nations games. His abrasive, all-action displays from the bench put Mefin Davies under pressure for his place throughout the tournament. An experienced international, he was the perfect replacement for Mefin in the final stages of the game and his undoubted strength and scrummaging savvy were fundamental to the huge forward effort against France in the final quarter.

2005 RBS 6 Nations: Italy (r), France (r), Scotland (r), Ireland (r)
Points: 0

Jonathan Thomas

Club: Ospreys
Born: 27.12.82, Pembroke
Position: Lock
Height: 1.96m
Weight: 106kg

Jonathan Thomas played his part in four games in the Grand Slam campaign. Replacing the injured Dafydd Jones, Thomas started on the blindside against Italy and celebrated the call-up by crashing over to score Wales' first try against the Azzurri, after latching on to a long pass from Michael Owen. In the loose he was equally effective and finished the game as Wales' top tackler. His versatility meant he could cover any of the back five positions and he proved a more than competent deputy whenever called upon.

2005 RBS 6 Nations: England (r), Italy, France (r), Ireland (r)
Points: 5 – 1T

John Yapp

Club: Blues
Born: 09.04.83, Bridgend
Position: Prop
Height: 1.88m
Weight: 122kg

John Yapp's eye-catching appearances in this year's competition as an impact replacement saw him keep a player of Duncan Jones' quality out of the 22. He made his debut against England, deep into the second half – making his presence felt immediately as he bulldozed towards the England line – and appeared in every one of the 2005 Six Nations games, usually replacing Adam Jones when Gethin Jenkins switches to tighthead. His strong scrummaging and telling contributions in the loose made a telling impression.

2005 RBS 6 Nations: England (r), Italy (r), France (r), Scotland (r), Ireland (r)
Points: 0

Gareth Cooper

Club: Dragons
Born: 07.05.79, Bridgend
Position: Scrum-half
Height: 1.71m
Weight: 84kg

Dwayne Peel currently holds the upper hand in Wales' competitive battle for the scrum-half jersey, although Gareth Cooper was first choice for the role before he was hit by injury prior to the Autumn Series. He took part in the first three games of the tournament and made an immediate impression against England, where his break and grubber kick put the pressure on Jason Robinson – who subsequently gave away the penalty that allowed Henson to win the game. He missed the last two games after injuring an ankle playing in the Tsunami Aid game at Twickenham.

2005 RBS 6 Nations: England, Italy (r), France (r)
Points: 0

Robin Sowden-Taylor

Club: Blues
Born: 09.06.82, Cardiff
Position: Flanker
Height: 1.85m
Weight: 96kg

Robin Sowden-Taylor made his Wales debut against Italy – playing in the last five minutes after replacing club-mate Martyn Williams. One for the future, Sowden-Taylor is shaping up to be an ideal replacement for his Blues colleague.

2005 RBS 6 Nations: Italy (r)
Points: 0

Mark Taylor

Club: Scarlets
Born: 27.02.73, Blaenavon
Position: Wing
Height: 1.83m
Weight: 96kg

Mark Taylor was not expected to make the final 22 for the Ireland game, but as a result of injuries to Hal Luscombe and Rhys Williams, he started on the wing. The hard-hitting centre filled in heroically in the unfamiliar role, nullifying Denis Hickie's attacking forays.

2005 RBS 6 Nations: Ireland
Points: 0

Ceri Sweeney

Club: Dragons
Born: 21.01.80, Pontypridd
Position: Fly-half
Height: 1.78m
Weight: 86kg

Ceri Sweeney was a fine replacement for Wales throughout the Six Nations. The chirpy back is able to cover both outside-half and inside-centre, offering the squad some real versatility. He came on as a replacement against Italy, France and Scotland.

2005 RBS 6 Nations: Italy (r), France (r), Scotland (r)
Points: 0

Hal Luscombe

Club: Dragons
Born: 23.02.81, Laingfburg, South Africa
Position: Wing
Height: 1.91m
Weight: 99kg

Hal Luscombe had a relatively quiet campaign. A starter on the wing against England, he also played against Italy, where he showed his flair with some fine breaks. Injury forced him off at Stadio Flaminio and he played no further part in the competition.

2005 RBS 6 Nations: England, Italy, Scotland (r)
Points: 0

Ian Gough

Club: Dragons
Born: 10.11.76, Pontypool
Position: Lock
Height: 1.96m
Weight: 110kg

The tough-tackling Dragons lock proved a reliable replacement, filling Brent Cockbain's sizable boots for the last 15 minutes of the Italy game. He was unfortunate not to add further to his tally of international caps.

2005 RBS 6 Nations: Italy (r)
Points: 0

Dafydd Jones

Club: Scarlets
Born: 24.06.79, Aberystwyth
Position: Flanker
Height: 1.90m
Weight: 108kg

Dafydd was one of Wales' fallen heroes. He only played in the opening game against England – a groin injury in the 66th minute ruling him out for the rest of the tournament. Until then, he had been tireless in the rucks and mauls and tackled relentlessly.

2005 RBS 6 Nations: England
Points: 0

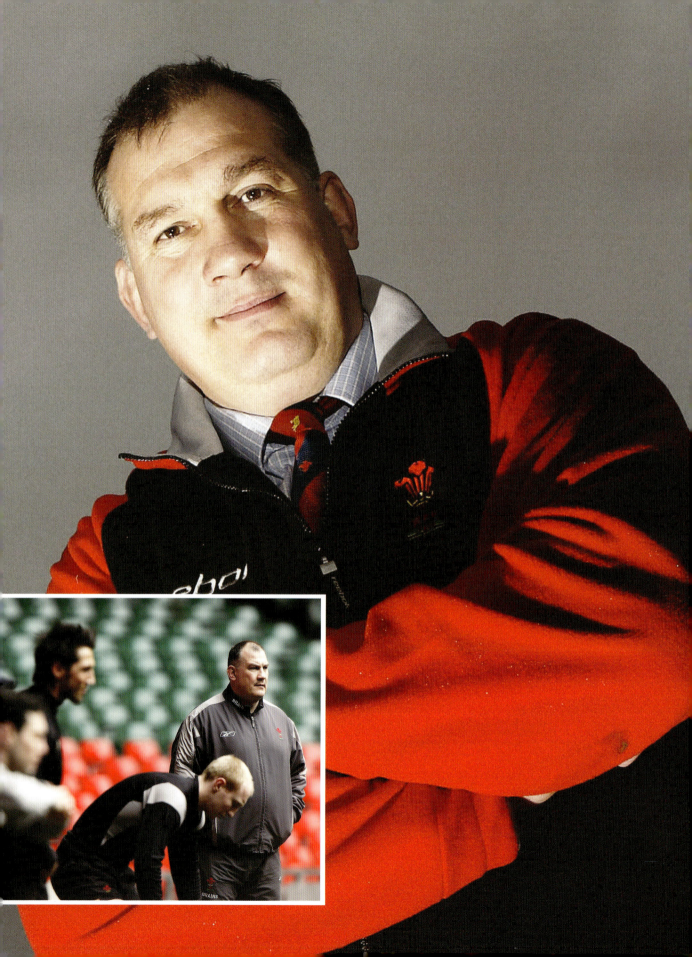

Forward thinking

Although few would deny that Wales' triumph has been a team effort, one man was charged with setting the course

Mike Ruddock's Welsh coaching career has got off to a flying start. After missing out on Wales' top coaching job in 1995 and 1998, he has already achieved what no Welsh coach has managed for 27 years; namely winning a Grand Slam. Ruddock has scaled the heights of Six Nations success by ensuring that Wales delivered on set-pieces and had a powerful pack capable of punching holes in the loose. A proud Celt, he is also credited with instiling a Welshness back into the squad; something that was absent in the All Black coaching years.

Ruddock first took the helm in May 2004, after former coach Steve Hansen had returned to New Zealand. His tenure started with an impressive victory against the Barbarians, with Wales running out 42-0 winners. From there, it was out to South America for a Test series against the rugged Pumas. Despite missing several experienced squad members including Gareth Thomas and Stephen Jones, Wales tied the two-match series. They finished off the summer tour with a tough Test at altitude against a rampant South Africa, which they lost 53-18. In the Autumn Series, performances and results were much improved, with thumping victories over Romania and Japan and, more significantly, the narrowest of losses to New Zealand and South Africa.

As a player, Ruddock was an abrasive, free-scoring flanker who gained a Wales B cap in 1982 and was thought to be on the verge of a full Welsh cap. His club career took him from his home town of Blaina to Tredegar and finally to Swansea, where he excelled with 43 tries in 119 appearances, earning a runners-up medal in the 1983 Welsh Cup. In 1985, Ruddock's playing career came crashing to a halt. An electricity linesman by trade, he suffered a fractured skull, compressed three vertebrae in his back and damaged an organ of balance in one ear after being knocked down from a pole. After two months lying prostrate in hospital, the doctors insisted he end his playing days. He was just 27.

Forever a fighter, Ruddock tried to regain his fitness by running on the hard roads around Blaina, only to further injure his back. He took to training on the more forgiving grass at the rugby club, where he was asked to help out with the forwards coaching. He realised he had an aptitude for the job and was given the coaching role for the following season. From Blaina he continued his apprenticeship at Cross Keys, before heading over the Irish Sea to Bective Rangers in 1990 for a year. Luckily for Ruddock, he heard that Swansea were looking for a coach, and it wasn't long before he was back at his former club, eventually becoming director of coaching.

In 1997, he again moved across the Irish Sea to Leinster where he was director of coaching until 2000 and involved with Brian Ashton in the Ireland A set up. It was at Leinster that he gave Ireland captain Brian O'Driscoll his first professional contract.

Sensing that he needed to return to Wales to enhance his chances of coaching his country, he took up a coaching position with Ebbw Vale and led them to two Welsh Cup semi-finals. When the club merged with Newport to form the Newport Gwent Dragons, he drove them to second place in the Celtic League despite a dearth of big name "stars". He was previously involved with the WRU, coaching Emerging Wales and Wales A, and was assistant coach to Alec Evans in the 1995 Rugby World Cup. His honours include winning the Heineken League with Swansea in 1992 and 1994, the Welsh Cup in 1995 and the Irish Provincial Championships in 1997 with Leinster. The highlight of his club coaching career was with Swansea, when they beat the reigning world champions Australia 21-6 in 1992.

In leading Wales to a Grand Slam in 2005, he became the first coach to spearhead a side to a Six Nations championship by winning three away games, including the undoubted comeback of the tournament in the sensational game against France.

RBS 6 NATIONS
Other fixtures

France v Scotland	100
Italy v Ireland	102
Scotland v Ireland	104
England v France	106
Scotland v Italy	108
Ireland v England	110
Ireland v France	112
England v Italy	114
Italy v France	116
England v Scotland	118

France 16 Scotland 9

Stade de France
Saturday, February 5, 2005
Attendance: 78,750

France		Scotland
Pepito Elhorga	15	Chris Paterson
Aurelien Rougerie	14	Simon Danielli
Damien Traille	13	Andy Craig
Brian Liebenberg	12	Hugo Southwell
Christophe Dominici	11	Sean Lamont
Yann Delaigue	10	Dan Parks
Pierre Mignoni	9	Chris Cusiter
Sylvian Marconnet	1	Tom Smith
William Servat	2	Gordon Bulloch (c)
Pieter De Villiers	3	Gavin Kerr
Fabien Pelous (c)	4	Stuart Grimes
Jerome Thion	5	Scott Murray
Julien Bonnaire	6	Jason White
Patrick Tabacco	7	Allister Hogg
Sebastien Chabal	8	Jon Petrie

Replacements: Ludovic Valbon for Rougerie (18), Olivier Milloud for De Villiers (52), Yannick Nyanga for Tabacco (64), Gregory Lamboley for Thion (70), Frederic Michalak for Delaigue (74), Sebastien Bruno for Servat (80), Dimitri Yachvili for Valbon (80)
Try: Traille **Con:** Michalak
Pens: Delaigue 2
Drop Goal: Delaigue

Replacements: Bruce Douglas for Kerr (55), Nathan Hines for Murray (66), Jon Dunbar for Petrie (80)
Sin Bin: Petrie (71)
Pens: Paterson 3

Referee: Nigel Williams (Wales)

"We were robbed blind," stated Scotland's Australian coach Matt Williams after a heart-breaking, injury-time defeat to a French side that barely offered a credible threat for the preceding 80 minutes. It was, all evidence permitting, a response that owed more to emotion than reason. His principal gripe was that Allister Hogg was adjudged to have placed a heel in touch before scrambling over in the right-hand corner for a potentially match-winning try. Television replays and plenty of hindsight indicate that the touch-judge probably made the right call. A more legitimate complaint may have been made about the late sin-binning of Jon Petrie for an offside that clearly was not his offence – making the "deliberate" element required for an expulsion all the more unfortunate. As it was, Scotland were down to 14 men when France, in the dying seconds, made their sole impression on the Scottish defence; in the final minute, Hugo Southwell's clearing kick was charged down and Damien Traille won the race to the line and forced the ball down for the match-stealing score.

It was heart-breaking for the Scots. In the early stages of the second half they had led 9-0 through three Chris Paterson penalties, one the direct result of a superb break by Chris Cuister. But the lead was clawed back through two penalties by Yann Delaigue, who then slotted over an equalising drop-goal immediately following Petrie's late dismissal. Although they could take considerable heart from a performance that was as exuberant as it was committed, failing to convert territorial supremacy into a victory can only prove costly at this level of rugby. They might not have a better chance of beating the French in their own backyard for some considerable time.

Italy 17 Ireland 28

Stadio Flaminio
Sunday, February 6, 2005
Attendance: 25,000

Italy		Ireland
Roland de Marigny	15	Geordan Murphy
Mirco Bergamasco	14	Shane Horgan
Gonzalo Canale	13	Brian O'Driscoll (c)
Andrea Masi	12	Gordan D'Arcy
Ludovico Nitoglia	11	Denis Hickie
Luciano Orquera	10	Ronan O'Gara
Alessandro Troncon	9	Peter Stringer
Andrea Lo Cicero	1	Reggie Corrigan
Fabio Ongaro	2	Shane Byrne
Leandro Castrogiovanni	3	John Hayes
Santiago Dellape	4	Malcolm O'Kelly
Marco Bortolami (c)	5	Paul O'Connell
Aaron Persico	6	Simon Easterby
Mauro Bergamasco	7	Denis Leamy
Sergio Parisse	8	Anthony Foley

Replacements: Carlo Del Fava for Dellape (66), Kaine Robertson for Canale (71), Georgio Intoppa for Lo Cicero (78), Salvatore Perugini for Ongaro (78), David Dal Maso for Parisse (78)
Try: Castrogiovanni
Pens: Orquera, de Marigny 3

Replacements: Girvan Dempsey for D'Arcy (29), Marcus Horan for Corrigan (61), Frankie Sheahan for Byrne (77), Donncha O'Callaghan for O'Connell (77), Eric Miller for Foley (77)
Tries: Murphy, Stringer, Hickie
Con: O'Gara 2
Pens: O'Gara 3

Referee: Paddy O'Brien (New Zealand)

It was hardly the most convincing opening to what many were predicting would be Ireland's first Grand Slam in colour. Despite the strides Italy had made in recent years, not least at the 2003 World Cup, a trip to Rome is still regarded more as a pre-season friendly than a significant hurdle on the path to glory. And there was certainly an air of Irish complacency in the first half; the visitors appeared genuinely shocked by gutsy Italian tackling and fierce mauling. In fact, Ireland barely managed a meaningful passage of possession until Geordan Murphy made best use of Brian O'Driscoll's dummy and break, and dived over the line for the opening try on 28 minutes.

All Italy had for their dominance, though, was a string of Luciano Orquera penalties and even though the gap had narrowed to a solitary point at one stage, the Italian back division simply couldn't live with the pace and power of O'Driscoll. Another burst between the flailing centres on 49 minutes set up Denis Hickie and Shane Horgan, and a clever over-the-shoulder pass fell kindly for Peter Stringer to round off the move. Italy continued to pound away at the Irish pack, but with the inexperienced Orquera at fly-half, they rarely threatened to expose a defence that was prematurely shorn of Gordon D'Arcy, withdrawn following a hamstring pull. Even more worryingly for Ireland's title hopes, O'Driscoll was forced out of the game late on for similar reasons. Hickie's late try, after he had neatly exploited a midfield turnover, put some gloss on the scoreline, but there were more questions than answers for Irish fans as they trooped away from the Eternal City.

Scotland 13 Ireland 40

Murrayfield
Saturday, February 12, 2005
Attendance: 67,530

Scotland		Ireland
Chris Paterson	15	Geordan Murphy
Simon Danielli	14	Girvan Dempsey
Andrew Craig	13	Shane Horgan
Hugo Southwell	12	Kevin Maggs
Sean Lamont	11	Denis Hickie
Dan Parks	10	Ronan O'Gara
Chris Cusiter	9	Peter Stringer
Tom Smith	1	Reggie Corrigan
Gordon Bulloch (c)	2	Shane Byrne
Gavin Kerr	3	John Hayes
Stuart Grimes	4	Malcolm O'Kelly
Scott Murray	5	Paul O'Connell (c)
Jason White	6	Simon Easterby
Jon Petrie	7	Johnny O'Connor
Allister Hogg.	8	Anthony Foley.

Replacements: Mike Blair for Cusiter (71), Bruce Douglas for Kerr (71), Nathan Hines for Murray (71)
Tries: Southwell, Petrie
Pen: Paterson

Replacements: Eric Miller for O'Connor (66), Marcus Horan for Corrigan (72), Frankie Sheahan for Byrne (72), Gavin Duffy for Hickie (75), David Humphreys for O'Gara (75), Guy Easterby for Stringer (75), Donncha O'Callaghan for O'Kelly (75)
Tries: O'Kelly, O'Connell, Hickie, Hayes, Duffy
Cons: O'Gara 2, Humphreys
Pens: O'Gara 3

Referee: Joël Jutge (France)

For about 10 minutes, it seemed as though the opening weekend's games had betrayed more about these two teams than many were prepared to believe; Scotland cut loose from deep, were electric at the breakdown and harried the Irish half-backs into a string of unforced errors, while Ireland, shorn of the centre pairing of Brian O'Driscoll and Gordon D'Arcy, appeared shell-shocked that one of the lesser Six Nations sides should dare seek to dent their title aspirations. As such, Scotland bolted into an early lead with a sweeping move started by Chris Paterson, carried on by Andy Craig and finished by Hugo Southwell. Murrayfield was in raptures. If only briefly.

The mood of celebration disintegrated as rapidly as the Scottish defence, and after a couple of quick penalties by Ronan O'Gara, Malcolm O'Kelly — who was in the midst of surpassing Mike Gibson's Irish caps record — collected a lineout and was shunted over the line by a voracious pack. The lead, extended further by another O'Gara penalty, was insurmountable when Paul O'Connell barged over, following a punishing tap-penalty charge by Anthony Foley. The half-time interval offered the smallest respite as Ireland continued their onslaught in the second period, and Denis Hickie sprinted away to open up a 15-point lead. Jon Petrie at least kept Scotland interested with a try in the corner, but late scores from giant prop John Hayes and new arrival Gavin Duffy, in only his second Test, rubbed salt into deepening Scottish wounds. Ireland's title hopes were buoyant, while Scotland were once again left to search for Italy's results at the other end of the table.

England 17 France 18

Twickenham
Saturday, February 13, 2005
Attendance: 75,000

England		France
Jason Robinson (c)	15	Pepito Elhorga
Mark Cueto	14	Christophe Dominici
Jamie Noon	13	Brian Liebenberg
Olly Barkley	12	Damien Traille
Josh Lewsey	11	Jimmy Marlu
Charlie Hodgson	10	Yann Delaigue
Harry Ellis	9	Dimitri Yachvili
Graham Rowntree	1	Sylvain Marconnet
Steve Thompson	2	Sebastien Bruno
Phil Vickery	3	Nicholas Mas
Danny Grewcock	4	Fabien Pelous (c)
Ben Kay	5	Jerome Thion
Joes Worsley	6	Serge Betsen
Lewis Moody	7	Julien Bonnaire
Martin Corry	8	Sebastien Chabal

Replacements: Ben Cohen for Cueto (74), Matt Dawson for Ellis (79)
Tries: Barkley, Lewsey
Cons: Hodgson 2
Pens: Hodgson

Replacements: Jean-Philippe Grandclaude for Marlu (43), William Servat for Bruno (49), Olivier Milloud for Mas (49), Yannick Nyanga for Chabal (49), Frederic Michalak for Delaigue (67), Gregory Lamboley for Pelous (80)
Pens: Vachvili 6

Referee: Paddy O'Brien (New Zealand)

Although few could doubt that England were unlucky to lose to a faltering, fragile French side, there must also have been the sense that the World Champions had been hoisted with their own petard – the occasions when England have fashioned victory against superior opposition through little more than the accuracy of their fly-half's boot are too many to recall. Perhaps even more ironic was that England not only out-scored the French two tries to nil at Twickenham, but that they missed no less than six penalties – and still had time to fluff a last-minute drop-goal from Jonny Wilkinson's replacement, Charlie Hodgson. The arch-pragmatists had been undone by uncharacteristic sloppiness in the game's fundamentals.

As it was, Dimitri Yachvili's half-dozen goals, four of them in the second period, saw the French squeak past the hosts and thoroughly ruin Andy Robinson's home Six Nations debut. Coming so soon after the two-point defeat in Cardiff, the new coach was experiencing just how cruel international rugby can be.

In the first-half, though, it must have seemed the easiest game in the world. England scored two exceptional tries, the first from Olly Barkley, who benefited from a piercing Jamie Noon break, and the second from Josh Lewsey, who underlined his increasing star status with a dashing finish on the left wing.

The 17-6 half-time lead seemed secure enough. But then came the wastefulness, and back came the French. A comprehensive back-line reshuffle was complimented by the introduction of William Servat up front and they started to put England on the back foot. The penalties were conceded and, when they were coolly slotted, England had no answer.

Scotland 18 Italy 10

Murrayfield
Saturday, February 26, 2005
Attendance: 48,145

Scotland		Italy
Chris Paterson	15	Roland de Marigny
Simon Webster	14	Mirco Bergamasco
Andrew Craig	13	Cristian Stoica
Hugo Southwell	12	Andrea Masi
Sean Lamont	11	Ludovico Nitoglia
Dan Parks	10	Luciano Orquera
Chris Cusiter	9	Alessandro Troncon
Tom Smith	1	Andrea Lo Cicero
Gordon Bulloch (c)	2	Fabio Ongaro
Gavin Kerr	3	Martin Castrogiovanni
Stuart Grimes	4	Santiago Dellape
Scott Murray	5	Marco Bortolami (c)
Simon Taylor	6	Aaron Persico
Jon Petrie	7	David Dal Maso
Allister Hogg	8	Sergio Parisse

Replacements: Ben Hinshelwood for Southwell (71), Bruce Douglas for Kerr (73), Nathan Hines for Murray (75), Jon Dunbar for Taylor (75), Mike Blair for Cusiter (80), Robbie Russell for Bulloch (80)
Pens: Paterson 6

Replacements: Roberto Pedrazzi for Masi (58), Salvatore Perugini for Castrogiovanni (63), Carlo Del Fava for Dellape (63), Paul Griffen for Orquera (68), Kaine Robertson for Bergamasco (73)
Try: Masi
Con: de Marigny
Pen: de Marigny

Referee: Stuart Dickinson (Australia)

The fixture that has, sadly for the proud Scots, become a contest for the wooden spoon in recent seasons went the way of the home side in a disjointed, largely forgettable afternoon. Characterised by long spells of punt-tennis and senseless turnovers, it was difficult to summon much in the way of a silver lining for a Scottish side that failed to unearth a try against the most porous defence in the competition – although the place-kicking and general quality of Chris Paterson remains a beacon amid the general mediocrity. Indeed, all of Scotland's points came from Paterson penalties, the only six he actually attempted. He could consider himself, alongside the rampaging winger Sean Lamont, unfortunate to miss out on the Lions tour to New Zealand.

It is a different story for Australian coach Matt Williams, who can look back on just three wins in 15 games – and those have come against Samoa, Japan and Italy. His patched-up side struggled to outmanoeuvre Italy's limited, forward-based approach, and ultimately he can be extremely grateful that Roland de Marigny squandered a hat-trick of penalties. For the Italians, consolation came with Andrea Masi's try two minutes from time after a clearing kick from Gordon Ross had been charged down – conjuring up memories of Paris on the opening weekend. A home win, but little cheer for the Murrayfield faithful.

Ireland 19 England 13

Landsdowne Road
Sunday, February 27, 2005
Attendance: 48,200

Ireland		England
Geordan Murphy	15	Jason Robinson (c)
Girvan Dempsey	14	Mark Cueto
Brian O'Driscoll (c)	13	Jamie Noon
Shane Horgan	12	Olly Barkley
Denis Hickie	11	Josh Lewsey
Ronan O'Gara	10	Charlie Hodgson
Peter Stringer	9	Harry Ellis
Reggie Corrigan	1	Graham Rowntree
Shane Byrne	2	Steve Thompson
John Hayes	3	Matt Stevens
Malcolm O'Kelly	4	Danny Grewcock
Paul O'Connell	5	Ben Kay
Simon Easterby	6	Joe Worsley
Johnny O'Connor	7	Lewis Moody
Anthony Foley	8	Martin Corry

Replacements: Marcus Horan for Corrigan (68)
Try: O'Driscoll
Con: O'Gara
Pens: O'Gara 2
Drop Goals: O'Gara 2

Replacements: Matt Dawson for Ellis (70)
Try: Corry
Con: Hodgson
Pen: Hodgson
Drop Goal: Hodgson

Referee: Jonathan Kaplan (South Africa)

"Three in a row" isn't an unfamiliar term to England fans. When it refers to victories, that is. For Andy Robinson, the close, controversial defeat to Ireland – by the exact same scoreline as last year, when the Irish inflicted a humiliating reverse at the usually impregnable Twickenham – meant that for the first time since 1987 England had lost a trio of Championship games. And the England coach was not remotely amused. Robinson claimed that his side had been robbed of two certain tries. The first was clearly the most galling: with half-time approaching and England trailing 12-10, Charlie Hodgson's cross-field punt was collected by Mark Cueto, who gleefully dived over the line. The referee, though, signalled that the winger was in front of the kicker at the point of contact and blew for offside – a judgement most observers, neutral or otherwise, concluded was extremely harsh. Then, in the dying minutes of the game, a rolling maul was forced over the line, with Josh Lewsey clutching the ball under his arm, only for the referee to rule for a five-metre scrum – to Ireland.

That said, England were still a long way from their fluent best, and the boot of Ronan O'Gara and a fleetfooted burst along the touchline from Brian O'Driscoll proved sufficient against a stuttering visiting attack. England's one try came from Martin Corry, who ran unchallenged from the base of a ruck before half-time. As such, it was another false dawn for Andy Robinson, and Ireland's title aspirations remained well and truly intact.

Ireland 19 France 26

Landsdowne Road
Sunday, March 12, 2005
Attendance: 49,250

Ireland		France
Geordan Murphy	15	Julien Laharrague
Girvan Dempsey	14	Cedric Heymans
Brian O'Driscoll (c)	13	Yannick Jauzion
Kevin Maggs	12	Benoit Baby
Denis Hickie	11	Christophe Dominici
Ronan O'Gara	10	Yann Delaigue
Peter Stringer	9	Dimitri Yachvili
Reggie Corrigan	1	Sylvain Marconnet
Shane Byrne	2	Sebastien Bruno
John Hayes	3	Nicholas Mas
Malcolm O'Kelly	4	Fabien Pelous (c)
Paul O'Connell	5	Jerome Thion
Simon Easterby	6	Serge Betsen
Johnny O'Connor	7	Yannick Nyanga
Anthony Foley	8	Julien Bonnaire

Replacements: Marcus Horan for Corrigan (71), Eric Miller for Foley (71)
Try: O'Driscoll
Con: O'Gara
Pens: O'Gara 4

Replacements: Pieter De Villiers for Mas (41), Gregory Lamboley for Nyanga (55), Frederic Michalak for Delaigue (70), Pascal Pape for Pelous (72), Dimitri Szarzewski for Bruno (77)
Tries: Dominici 2, Baby
Con: Yachvili
Pens: Yachvili 2
Drop Goal: Delaigue

Referee: Tony Spreadbury (England)

It was the scoreline that ensured there could be only one Grand Slam winner in 2005. Although the Championship and the Triple Crown were still up for grabs for the Irish, this late defeat to an inspired and resolute French side signalled an extension to the 57-year dream. France were, for the most part, several classes above the home side, and two tries in a first half in which they were playing into a strong headwind proved telling. The first came on the half hour courtesy of characteristic back-line flair, with debutant Benoît Baby linking with full-back Julien Laharrague to set up Christophe Dominici. If the first was a team effort, the second was down to the individual brilliance of Baby; the 21-year-old centre burst between Kevin Maggs and Girvan Dempsey to canter in unopposed from the halfway line. Still, three O'Gara penalties managed to keep Ireland within reach at the half, trailing 18-9, and that gap was reduced further by a fourth O'Gara penalty eight minutes into the second period. After exchanging further goals, a piece of individual brilliance from Brian O'Driscoll sent him clear and narrowed the margin to two points, and suddenly Irish eyes were widening at the prospect of a miracle comeback.

Hope was shortlived. As Malcolm Kelly raced into the maelstrom of French defenders, he was stripped of the ball and Dominici strolled almost apologetically to the line unchallenged to silence the Landsdowne Road faithful, while the clamour in Wales was reaching fever pitch.

England 39 Italy 7

Twickenham

Saturday, March 12, 2005

Attendance: 75,000

England		Italy
Iain Balshaw	15	Gert Peens
Mark Cueto	14	Roberto Pedrazzi
Jamie Noon	13	Matteo Barbini
Olly Barkley	12	Andrea Masi
Josh Lewsey	11	Ludovico Nitoglia
Charlie Hodgson	10	Luciano Orquera
Harry Ellis	9	Alessandro Troncon
Graham Rowntree	1	Andrea Lo Cicero
Steve Thompson	2	Fabio Ongaro
Matt Stevens	3	Salvatore Perugini
Danny Grewcock	4	Carlo Del Fava
Ben Kay	5	Marco Bortolami (c)
Joe Worsley	6	Aaron Persico
Lewis Moody	7	David Dal Maso
Martin Corry (c)	8	Sergio Parisse

Replacements: Matt Dawson for Ellis (51), Steve Borthwick for Grewcock (62), Ollie Smith for Noon (66), Andy Titterell for Thompson (66), Andy Goode for Hodgson (74), Duncan Bell for Rowntree (74), Andy Hazell for Worsley (74)
Tries: Cueto 3, Thompson, Balshaw, Hazell
Cons: Hodgson 2, Goode
Pen: Hodgson

Replacements: Giorgio Intoppa for Ongaro (20), Walter Pozzebon for Barbini (40), Sivio Orlando for Dal Maso (40)
Try: Troncon
Con: Peens

Referee: Mark Lawrence (South Africa)

It's rare to experience a Six Nations game at Twickenham with so little impact on the Championship, particularly with two rounds remaining. While Dublin and Cardiff became, for this season at least, the focal points of the game in the northern hemisphere, Andy Robinson's side gathered in south-west London looking to notch up their first win. After three narrow defeats – each of which could, with a little fortune, easily have been victories – a match against Italy was a much-needed rest-cure for ailing limbs and creaking confidences. A try in the first 10 minutes from Sale winger Mark Cueto sent England merrily on their way, although the spirited Italians ensured the expected cricket score never materialised. It wasn't until the 38th minute that England went over again, when Steve Thompson bulldozed his way to the line after Italy had conceded a scrum-22 with a wayward kick-off. Shortly afterwards, another kick-off infringement by the Italians handed possession back to England, and 11 phases later Cueto was over for his second.

After the interval, Italy rolled a maul past some shoddy England tackling to score through Alessandro Troncon, but three more England tries, from the outstanding Iain Balshaw, Cueto – for his hat-trick – and Andy Hazell, completed the rout. The nature of the opposition renders much evaluation of the performance redundant, but there was a look of youth about the England side that should give the rest of the Six Nations ample reason to fear Robinson's side next year.

Italy 13 France 56

Stadio Flaminio
Saturday, March 19, 2005
Attendance: 24,593

Italy		France
Gert Peens	15	Julien Laharrague
Kaine Robertson	14	Cedric Heymans
Andrea Masi	13	David Marty
Simon Picone	12	Yannick Jauzion
Ludovico Nitoglia	11	Christophe Dominici
Luciano Orquera	10	Yann Delaigue
Alessandro Troncon	9	Dimitri Yachvili
Andrea Lo Cicero	1	Sylvain Marconnet
Fabio Ongaro	2	Sebastien Bruno
Salvatore Perugini	3	Nicolas Mas
Santiago Dellape	4	Fabien Pelous (c)
Marco Bortolami (c)	5	Jerome Thion
Aaron Persico	6	Serge Betsen
David Dal Maso	7	Yannick Nyanga
Sergio Parisse	8	Julien Bonnaire

Replacements: Leandro Castrogiovanni for Lo Cicero (28), Carlo Festuccia for Ongaro (56), Paul Griffen for Troncon (59), Del Fava for Dellape (61), Roberto Pedrazzi for Robertson (67), Silvio Orlando for Dal Maso (73) **Sin Bin:** Bortolami (14) **Try:** Robertson **Con:** Peens **Pens:** Peens 2

Replacements: Damien Traille for Dominici (32), Pieter de Villiers for Mas (41), William Servat for Bruno (59), Frederic Michalak for Delaigue (61), Gregory Lamboley for Nyanga (66), Pierre Mignoni for Yachvili (70), Pascal Pape for Pelous (72) **Tries:** Nyanga, Jauzion, Laharrague, Marty 2, Lamboley, Mignoni **Cons:** Yachvili 4, Michalak 2 **Pens:** Yachvili 3

Referee: Donal Courtney (Ireland)

It was easy. In the end. France laboured underneath an unseasonably powerful Roman sun, and although victory was rarely in question, the visitors found it difficult to extend a 17-10 lead accrued in the early stages, and only settled the matter in the 66th minute when they scored their fourth try through the irrepressible David Marty. After that, it was a race to notch up the 43-point margin that would, in theory, put them in with a shout of the title should Ireland beat Wales by – calculators at the ready – more than 10 points, but less than 15. Judging by the joyless back-slapping that greeted each additional score, it was a likelihood few Frenchmen had bothered to entertain.

At least France had started as though they wanted to rack up a century. They had scored two tries in the opening 15 minutes, thanks largely to the dominance of Christophe Dominici over Kiwi-born counterpart Kaine Robertson, and clinical breaks ended up with the dynamic Yannick Nyanga and Yannick Jauzion scoring tries. However, the deluge was curtailed by an 80-yard Robertson interception – a small measure of retribution – and France only scored again on the brink of half-time, when Julien Laharrague squeezed over the line after neat interplay. Superior French fitness then proved telling, and tries in the last 15 minutes – from Marty twice, Gregory Lamboley and Pierre Mignoni – finessed the scoreline. It wasn't enough for the title, and at the final whistle, both camps were left ruing the missed opportunities of the 2005 Six Nations.

England 43 Scotland 22

Twickenham
Saturday, March 19, 2005
Attendance: 75,000

England		Scotland
Iain Balshaw	15	Chris Paterson
Mark Cueto	14	Rory Lamont
Jamie Noon	13	Andrew Craig
Olly Barkley	12	Hugo Southwell
Josh Lewsey	11	Sean Lamont
Charlie Hodgson	10	Gordon Ross
Harry Ellis	9	Mike Blair
Matt Stevens	1	Tom Smith
Steve Thompson	2	Gordon Bulloch (c)
Duncan Bell	3	Gavin Kerr
Danny Grewcock	4	Nathan Hines
Ben Kay	5	Scott Murray
Joe Worsley	6	Jason White
Lewis Moody	7	Allister Hogg
Martin Corry (c)	8	Simon Taylor

Replacements: Steve Borthwick for Kay (13), Ollie Smith for Balshaw (31), Andy Hazell for Moody (40), Mike Worsley for Bell (51), Matt Dawson for Ellis (65), Andy Titterell for Thompson (72), Andy Goode for Hodgson (76)
Tries: Noon 3, J Worsley, Lewsey, Ellis, Cueto
Cons: Hodgson 4

Replacements: Bruce Douglas for Smith (24), Stuart Grimes for Murray (33)
Tries: S Lamont, Craig, Taylor
Cons: Paterson 2
Pen: Paterson

Referee: Alain Rolland (Ireland)

One of the more regrettable by-products of the professional era is that the Calcutta Cup consistently fails to be the competitive, blood-and-thunder showpiece that made it one of the highlights of the Six Nations calendar. England are hardly the ruthlessly efficient machine of recent years, yet this game proved that Scotland, the France game notwithstanding, struggle to make an impression on the stronger nations even when undergoing a very public transition. For the Twickenham crowd, though, the changing of the guard appears to represent a precursor to another sustained era of success. Youth was to be found everywhere in the England ranks, with Jamie Noon notching a hat-trick, Mark Cueto adding to his try tally, and Olly Barkley and Harry Ellis both impressing. Even new boy Mike Worsley, a player who had barely time to meet the squad before pulling on the white shirt, scrummaged with power and purpose.

The scoring was evenly-spaced, with set-pieces creating the platform for a Noon brace inside 24 minutes as Scotland's defensive frailties at centre came to the fore. The third came via Joe Worsley, and the fourth, with just 33 minutes on the clock, came from Josh Lewsey after superb handling in the midfield. Immediately before the interval, though, Sean Lamont dived over for a face-saving score, and in a similar vein to their mini-revival against the Welsh, Scotland managed to quickly pile up 22 points through Andy Craig and No 8 Simon Taylor, who galloped 35 metres having intercepted a Harry Ellis pass. But England wrapped things up with scores from Ellis, Noon and Cueto. It was the biggest England total of the tournament and, in the circumstances, said less about the hosts than Matt Williams' hapless visitors.

Wales Grand Slams

After 27 years, the waiting is finally over. **Chris Deary** rummages deep into the rugby archives for a bit of misty-eyed nostalgia

Previous Page: Gareth Edwards celebrates his 50th cap against England in 1978. Above: George Travers' victorious 1908 team

1908

The first ever Welsh Grand Slam was not short on drama. The opening match against England was played in heavy fog, with the 25,000 spectators able to see little more than shadowy figures moving in the mist. The key figure in the game that became known as "the phantom football match" was Welsh fly-half Percy Bush, who scored nine points and contributed to several more. Next came a nail-biting win over Scotland at home, with Wales claiming victory by a single point after the referee had disallowed a last-minute Scottish try by Ian Geddes. And the final game against Ireland was just as close. With 10 minutes remaining the scores were locked at 5-5 before tries from Reg Gibbs and Johnnie Williams earned Wales their fifth Triple Crown. 1908 was the first year in which France were included in the fixture list and, although they were not officially part of the Championship until 1910, a 36-4 victory, which was achieved despite Gibbs being brought down by a football-style tackle as he was about to score a try, meant Wales had also won their first Grand Slam.

January 18, 1908
Bristol City AFC Ground
England 18 Wales 28
English scorers
Tries: John Birkett (2), Walter Lapage, Rupert Williamson
Cons: Alan Wood (2), Geoff Roberts
Welsh scorers
Tries: Rhys Gabe (2), Percy Bush, Billy Trew, Reg Gibbs
Cons: Bert Winfield (2), Percy Bush
Pen: Bert Winfield
Drop Goal: Percy Bush

February 1, 1908
St Helen's, Swansea
Wales 6 Scotland 5
Welsh scorers
Tries: Billy Trew, Johnnie Williams
Scottish scorers
Try: Alex Purves
Con: Ian Geddes

March 2, 1908
Cardiff Arms Park
Wales 36 France 4†
Welsh scorers
Tries: Reg Gibbs (4), Billy Trew (2), Teddy Morgan (2), Dick Jones
Cons: Bert Winfield (2) Reg Gibbs
Pen: Bert Winfield
French scorers
Drop Goal: Charles Vareilles

March 14, 1908
Balmoral, Belfast
Ireland 5 Wales 11
Irish scorers
Try: Herbert Aston
Con: Cecil Parke
Welsh scorers
Tries: Johnnie Williams (2), Reg Gibbs
Con: Bert Winfield

	P	W	D	L	F	A	Pts
Wales	3	3	0	0	45	28	6
Scotland	3	1	0	2	32	32	2
England	3	1	0	2	41	47	2
Ireland	3	1	0	2	24	35	2

NB: Drop Goal = 4 points. Try = 3 points
† France were not officially part of the Championship until 1910

1909

The 1909 Championship was shrouded in controversy, with Scotland cancelling their fixture against England because the latter had broken the amateur laws by paying extra money to the touring Australians and All Blacks. The game was eventually rearranged, but by the time it was played both sides had lost the chance of winning the Grand Slam after defeats to Wales: England without scoring, and Scotland in a repeat of the previous year's last-minute drama. The referee awarded Scotland a penalty at the death – unaware that Jack Bancroft had been knocked unconscious, he penalised him for not playing the ball. But George Cunningham missed the kick, which meant that when Wales beat Ireland in their final game, they became the first side to win the Triple Crown two years running. Another comfortable victory over France also meant they had picked up their second Grand Slam.

January 16, 1909
Cardiff Arms Park
Wales 8 England 0
Welsh scorers
Tries: Phil Hopkins, Johnnie Williams
Con: Jack Bancroft

February 6, 1909
Inverleith, Edinburgh
Scotland 3 Wales 5
Scottish scorers
Pen: George Cunningham
Welsh scorers
Try: Billy Trew
Con: Jack Bancroft

NB: Drop Goal = 4 points, try = 3 points
† France were not officially part of the Championship until 1910

February 23, 1909
Colombes, Paris
France 5† Wales 47
French scorers
Try: R Sagot
Con: Paul Mauriat
Welsh scorers
Tries: Billy Trew (3), Melville Baker (3), Johnnie Williams (2), JP Jones (2), Jim Watts
Cons: Jack Bancroft (6), Billy Trew

March 13, 1909
St Helen's, Swansea
Wales 18 Ireland 5
Welsh scorers
Tries: Phil Hopkins, JP Jones, Jim Watts, Billy Trew
Cons: Jack Bancroft (3)
Irish scorers
Try: Charles Thompson
Con: Cecil Parke

	P	W	D	L	F	A	Pts
Wales	3	3	0	0	31	8	6
Scotland	3	2	0	1	30	16	4
Ireland	3	1	0	2	13	38	2
England	3	0	0	3	19	31	0

1911

Defeat at Twickenham a year earlier had denied Wales a third consecutive Grand Slam, although they did win the Championship. Wales avenged that defeat with a 15-11 victory in the first game of 1911 and went on to register comfortable wins over Scotland, France and Ireland. The win over Scotland was by a record margin and was achieved with 25 second-half points. The final match against Ireland was a Triple Crown decider, and Wales won it without even conceding a point to their visitors to claim a third Triple Crown and Grand Slam in four years. But it would be 39 years before the Welsh tasted such success again.

January 21, 1911
St Helen's Swansea
Wales 15 England 11
Welsh scorers
Tries: Reg Gibbs, Ivor Morgan, Billy Spiller, Joe Pugsley
Pen: Fred Birt
English scorers
Tries: Alan Roberts, Alf Kewney, John Scholfield
Con: Douglas Lambert

February 4, 1911
Inverleith, Edinburgh
Scotland 10 Wales 32
Scottish scorers
Tries: Fred Turner, Jock Scott
Drop Goal: Pat Munro
Welsh scorers
Tries: Reg Gibbs (3), Billy Spiller (2), Johnnie Williams (2), Rhys Thomas
Con: Louis Dyke
Drop Goal: Billy Spiller

February 28, 1911
Parc des Princes, Paris
France 0 Wales 15
Welsh scorers
Tries: Ivor Morgan, Johnnie Williams, Dicky Owen
Cons: Jack Bancroft (2)

March 11, 1911
Cardiff Arms Park
Wales 16 Ireland 0
Welsh scorers
Tries: Tom Evans, Jim Webb, Reg Gibbs
Cons: Jack Bancroft (2)

NB: Drop Goal = 4 points, try = 3 points

	P	W	D	L	F	A	Pts
Wales	4	4	0	0	78	21	8
Ireland	4	3	0	1	44	31	6
England	4	2	0	2	61	26	4
France	4	1	0	3	21	92	2
Scotland	4	0	0	4	43	77	0

Above: Welsh winger Ken Jones stretches for the corner flag against Ireland at Landsdowne Road in 1952. Wales won 6-3

1950

Thirty-nine years had passed since their last Grand Slam and 14 since their last Championship win, but Wales got off to a good start in 1950 with an 11-5 win in front of a record crowd of more than 75,000 at Twickenham. An impressive forward display against Scotland two weeks later set up a Triple Crown decider against Ireland in Belfast and, as ever, it was tight. With three minutes left the scores were locked at 3-3 and the game looked certain to be heading for a draw when Ray Cale pounced on a poor clearance and set up Malcolm Thomas for the winning try. The Grand Slam was sealed with a comfortable win over France, although the game was tinged with sadness as a minute's silence was held for the victims of the Llandow air crash.

January 21, 1950
Twickenham
England 5 **Wales** 11
English scorers
Try: JV Murray
Con: Murray Hofmeyr
Welsh scorers
Tries: Cliff Davies, Roy Cale
Con: Lewis Jones
Pen: Lewis Jones

February 4, 1950
St Helen's, Swansea
Wales 12 **Scotland** 0
Welsh scorers
Tries: Malcolm Thomas, Ken Jones
Pen: Lewis Jones
Drop Goal: Billy Cleaver

March 11, 1950
Ravenhill, Belfast
Ireland 3 **Wales** 6
Irish scorers
Pen: George Norton
Welsh scorers
Tries: Ken Jones, Malcolm Thomas

March 25, 1950
Cardiff Arms Park
Wales 21 **France** 0
Welsh scorers
Tries: Ken Jones (2), Roy John, Jack Matthews
Cons: Lewis Jones (3)
Pen: Lewis Jones

NB: Try = 3 points

	P	W	D	L	F	A	Pts
Wales	4	4	0	0	50	8	8
Scotland	4	2	0	2	21	49	4
Ireland	4	1	1	2	27	12	3
France	4	1	1	2	14	35	3
England	4	1	0	3	22	30	2

Above: Alun Thomas kicks the ball away against Scotland at the Arms Park in 1952. Wales ended up winning the game 11-0.

1952

When Wales were six points down and reduced to 14 men because of an injury to Lewis Jones in their first match against England at Twickenham, the Grand Slam seemed a long way away. But two tries from Olympic sprinter Ken Jones capped a memorable fight back and set the standard for the rest of the Championship. In the second game Wales revenged the previous year's "Murrayfield Massacre", when they had lost 19-0 to Scotland, and despite unconvincing performances in the final two games against Ireland and France, a ninth Triple Crown and fifth Grand Slam were secured.

January 19, 1952
Twickenham
England 6 Wales 8
English scorers
Tries: Albert Agar, Ted Woodward
Welsh scorers
Tries: Ken Jones (2)
Con: Malcolm Thomas

February 2, 1952
Cardiff Arms Park
Wales 11 Scotland 0
Welsh scorers
Try: Ken Jones
Con: Malcolm Thomas
Pens: Malcolm Thomas (2)

NB: Try = 3 points

March 8, 1952
Lansdowne Road
Ireland 3 Wales 14
Irish scorers
Pen: Gerry Murphy
Welsh scorers
Tries: RCC Thomas, Ken Jones, Rees Stephens
Con: Lewis Jones Pen: Lewis Jones

March 22, 1952
St Helen's, Swansea
Wales 9 France 5
Welsh scorers
Pens: Lewis Jones (2)
Drop Goal: Alun Thomas
French scorers
Try: Michel Pomathios
Con: Jean Prat

	P	W	D	L	F	A	Pts
Wales	4	4	0	0	42	14	8
England	4	3	0	1	34	14	6
Ireland	4	2	0	2	26	33	4
France	4	1	0	3	29	37	2
Scotland	4	0	0	4	22	55	0

1971

Even an injury to JPR Williams, sustained when he ran into Gareth Edwards, couldn't stop Wales extending their unbeaten run against England to eight years when they opened the 1971 Championship with a 22-6 win at Cardiff Arms Park. The next game against Scotland was a much closer affair, with Wales snatching victory by one point with just two minutes remaining, when John Taylor converted Gerald Davies' try from the touchline. The Triple Crown was sealed amid a party atmosphere at the Arms Park as the crowd ran on to congratulate their team after every score against the Irish. The Grand Slam, though, would have to be sealed in Paris, where the Welsh hadn't won for 14 years. That trend was reversed thanks to a brilliant try from Gareth Edwards that was set up by a magnificent 70-yard run from JPR Williams and a Barry John try that allowed him to equal Keith Jarrett's record of 31 points throughout the competition.

January 16, 1971
Cardiff Arms Park
Wales 22 England 6
Welsh scorers
Tries: Gerald Davies (2), John Bevan
Cons: John Taylor (2)
Drop Goals: Barry John (2)
Pen: JPR Williams
English scorers
Try: Charlie Hannaford
Pen: Peter Rossborough

February 6, 1971
Murrayfield
Scotland 18 Wales 19
Scottish scorers
Tries: Sandy Carmichael, Chris Rea
Pens: Peter Brown (4)
Welsh scorers
Tries: John Taylor, Gareth Edwards, Barry John, Gerald Davies
Cons: Barry John, John Taylor
Pen: Barry John

March 13, 1971
Cardiff Arms Park
Wales 23 Ireland 9
Welsh scorers
Tries: Gerald Davies (2), Gareth Edwards (2)
Con: Barry John
Pens: Barry John (2)
Drop Goal: Barry John
Irish scorers
Pens: Mike Gibson (3)

March 27, 1971
Colombes, Paris
France 5 Wales 9
French scorers
Try: Benoit Dauga
Con: Pierre Villepreux
Welsh scorers
Tries: Gareth Edwards, Barry John
Pen: Barry John

NB: Try = 3 points

	P	W	D	L	F	A	Pts
Wales	4	4	0	0	73	38	8
France	4	1	2	1	41	40	4
Ireland	4	1	1	2	41	46	3
England	4	1	1	2	44	58	3
Scotland	4	1	0	3	47	64	2

1976

A superb individual performance from JPR Williams inspired Wales to a record victory at Twickenham. That was followed by an equally impressive win over Scotland, a match remembered as "The Great Gag Match" because the Welsh players were banned from giving interviews owing to press criticism of the WRU's decision to leave Phil Bennett out of the England game. Bennett returned to the side to score 13 points and then went on to score more than half of Wales' points as they won at Lansdowne Road for the first time in 12 years, despite death threats from terrorist extremists prior to the game. With the Triple Crown won, Bennett took his Championship tally to a record 38 points in a tight finale against the French in which Mervyn Davies bravely played on through injury.

NB: Try = 4 points

January 17, 1976
Twickenham
England 9 Wales 21
English scorers
Pens: Alastair Hignall (3)
Welsh scorers
Tries: JPR Williams (2), Gareth Edwards
Cons: Steve Fenwick (3)
Pen: Allan Martin

February 7, 1976
Cardiff Arms Park
Wales 28 Scotland 6
Welsh scorers
Tries: JJ Williams, Gareth Edwards, Trevor Evans
Cons: Phil Bennett (2)
Pens: Phil Bennett (3)
Drop Goal: Steve Fenwick
Scottish scorers
Try: Andy Irvine
Con: Douglas Morgan

February 21, 1976
Lansdowne Road
Ireland 9 Wales 34
Irish scorers
Pens: Barry McGann (3)
Welsh scorers
Tries: Gerald Davies (2), Gareth Edwards, Phil Bennett
Cons: Phil Bennett (3)
Pens: Phil Bennett (3), Allan Martin

March 6, 1976
Cardiff Arms Park
Wales 19 France 13
Welsh scorers
Try: JJ Williams
Pens: Phil Bennett (2), Steve Fenwick (2), Allan Martin
French scorers
Tries: Jean-Francois Gourdon, Jean-Luc Averous
Con: Jean-Pierre Romeu
Pen: Jean-Pierre Romeu

	P	W	D	L	F	A	Pts
Wales	4	4	0	0	102	37	8
France	4	3	0	1	82	37	6
Scotland	4	2	0	2	49	59	4
Ireland	4	1	0	3	31	87	2
England	4	0	0	4	42	86	0